MOMMING HARD.

NORMALIZING THE HARD STUFF IN THE BEAUTIFUL CONTRAST OF MOTHERHOOD

Courtney St Croix & the Co-Author Team:

Alexandra Brown, Amanda Gurman, Andrea France, Barbara Parker, Brooke Shaugnessey, Carly Riding, Darci Prince, Elizabeth Cook, Elizabeth Desrocher-O'Quinn, Heather Hutchings, Jennifer Weare, Jen Hoffmeister, Jessica Mancuso, Laura McLeod, Lisa Colalillo, Lisa Southall, Melissa Stentiford, Michelle Hughes, Nicky Nock, Renae Fieck, Sabrina Martelli, Sarah Power Smith, Sharana Ali, Shauna Clark

LEADher.
PUBLISHING

MOMMING HARD
Normalizing the Hard Stuff in the Beautiful Contrast of Motherhood

MOMMING HARD
2021 LeadHer Publishing

Cover Design — Christina Williams
Interior Design — Christina Williams

ISBN: 978-1-7770177-6-7

For more information, visit www.lead-her.com
instagram.com/leadherpublishing
or email admin@lead-her.com

Praise for MOMMING HARD

"I love this book! It sums up motherhood so perfectly and is so relatable. We go through SO MUCH as mothers and the less we worry about expectations, rules, opinions, comparing and guilt the easier it will be. This book helps solidify that."

— **Jasmine Makela**

"The only word for the first part about your daughter is....chills. I was wiping the tears away because I can feel your pain, and even though I have not had the same experience, I understand how you felt. This book is going to be so helpful for all moms."

— **Ashley Zimmers**

"This book is a great reminder of the reality that things don't always go according to plan and that life and motherhood is truly an overwhelming balancing act as we juggle being a mom, wife, partner, lover, friend, daughter, sister, employee, professional and entrepreneur (in no particular order). In MOMMING HARD, we're called to return to the most important role we have — that of being a woman and embracing our own self-love, self-acceptance and self-nurturing which makes navigating all the other roles in life that much easier. I loved this anthology!"

— **Julia Aitken**

"I am happy to have found a book that relates to me as a mom, and particularly as a mom who also lives with ADD. The authors truly connect with us and cheer us on! It's raw and truthful."

— **Jen Parker**

Contents

INTRODUCTION

Courtney St Croix

AUTHOR PHOTO: ASHLEY ADAMS, FLASHBACK PHOTO CO
FIND COURTNEY: **@LEADHER_INC @LEADHERPUBLISHING**

Prior to becoming a mother myself, I had very few people in my circle who had already crossed that milestone. Well, I suppose "very few" is an exaggeration; I could probably better describe the level of mom-fluence in my life as "almost none." In the direct vicinity of my twenty-something, carefree life, I had my own mom of course, and my sister who was a new mom in 2011. That was basically it. I wouldn't describe myself as a "kid person" and, as far as I can remember, my childhood experience didn't include memories of dreaming, preparing, or longing to be a mom.

I'd never had a conversation with anybody about the level of difficulty "momming" could be potentially aligned with. It isn't necessarily energy to get down and dirty with "real-talk" as they were passing me on the way to the gym daycare? Was it because they refused to admit that they, too, were having a hard time parenting and that shoving their real feelings down was easier than admitting struggle? I don't know. I don't know the answers to these things, but what I *do* know is that I'm not the only one who has (not *had*, has, present tense, to be clear) hard, challenging, difficult, irritating, frustrating, and cry-inducing experiences while mothering, just like I have *hard*, challenging, difficult, irritating, frustrating and cry-inducing experiences IN MANY OTHER AREAS OF MY LIFE. Of this, I am certain. This book is filled with twenty-five examples of living evidence that I am not the only one. The purpose of this book is to allow you to see that you're not the only one, either.

Everything in life has a flip side. It goes without saying that any long-term experience you have in life is likely to have a few ups and downs along the way; sometimes they're quick and resolve easily, and other times they're more like phases of discomfort that are tricky to navigate. For some reason, there's a fear of sharing anything on the "down" side of parenting. Don't misread me: I love my child, and I am grateful for her every single day. We have incredibly beautiful moments together. She has 100% changed our lives for the better. She teaches me to do better every single day. She challenges me in good ways, too. My daughter, my partner, and myself are without a doubt the most important priorities in my life. I would do anything for them both and I wouldn't trade motherhood for the world. Hey, I know this is the way you feel too, so don't worry. I also know that as an emotionally-charged human you probably feel it's necessary to share this classic disclaimer to precede any complaining, too. Am I right? For what it's worth, acknowledging that you are having a difficult time and then admitting that parenting is hard does not discredit the amount of love you have for your child(ren). One does not cancel out the other. It's okay to admit that some days are hard. We're conditioned to believe that if we complain about

INTRODUCTION

Courtney St Croix

AUTHOR PHOTO: ASHLEY ADAMS, FLASHBACK PHOTO CO
FIND COURTNEY: **@LEADHER_INC @LEADHERPUBLISHING**

Prior to becoming a mother myself, I had very few people in my circle who had already crossed that milestone. Well, I suppose "very few" is an exaggeration; I could probably better describe the level of mom-fluence in my life as "almost none." In the direct vicinity of my twenty-something, carefree life, I had my own mom of course, and my sister who was a new mom in 2011. That was basically it. I wouldn't describe myself as a "kid person" and, as far as I can remember, my childhood experience didn't include memories of dreaming, preparing, or longing to be a mom.

I'd never had a conversation with anybody about the level of difficulty "momming" could be potentially aligned with. It isn't necessarily an appropriate topic of discussion to have with your own mother (lol, #awkward!) and when my sister was in the thick of the newborn stage, I could certainly gather that it wasn't *easy*, but there is just no way anyone who *is* a mother can explain to someone who *isn't yet* a mother just how hard it is, and why. Inside the beauty and gratitude you feel for having this brand new being in your life, there are hard pieces that aren't commonly discussed. To that end, they most certainly aren't discussed with someone who hasn't yet been through it themselves, nor with someone who has forgotten how difficult the stage is that you're currently in. Not to mention, you've been blessed with a beautiful child and you're just trying to get by and do your best. You don't want to burden anyone else with your complaints. You don't want to sound like you're an ungrateful bummer in the otherwise neutral dialogue, and it certainly isn't your MO to casually vent about your challenging experiences to friends and family when they ask you how things are going at Thanksgiving dinner.

So we don't. We do what society has deemed appropriate. We don't complain. We don't say much. We veil real emotions, stuff down our truth, and smile and nod.

Why yes, Aunt Susan, everything's going SO great!

Similarly, talking about how motherhood can be f*cking hard is not the kind of thing that gets casually mentioned in the mommy-and-me yoga class on Wednesday mornings. I can recall that we certainly discussed our babies, but it was rare that we centred the conversation on ourselves and how we were doing mentally, physically, and emotionally — especially if "not good" was our honest truth. Everybody just kind of...put on a good face. The worst anybody (including myself) would share was that we were "tired." I think we all knew that "tired" was a code word for a myriad of less-than-positive emotions and experiences, but tired was the only descriptor anyone felt comfortable enough to share, without the fear of judgement or appearing ungrateful — at least in a big group setting. I *can* recall having more private, one-on-one discussions about how I was going through something difficult, but there was always an element of shame and guilt painted with a tone of secrecy in those conversations.

I think it's more common to speak generally (and openly, truthfully) about how any new adventure in life comes with its own set of highs and lows, peaks and valleys, and waves of good versus bad — but when it comes to motherhood, it doesn't seem to be as simple of a conversation. When it comes to something like starting a new job, working on a relationship, making a big move — heck, even attempting to reach a fitness goal — all of these "journeys" in life are well-known, and it's socially acceptable for us to share something frustrating about the experience. We can open up about something hard at work, talk about a difficult phase in a relationship, or complain about missing a milestone at the gym — and do so without feeling guilty and fearing judgement about the pessimism.

In my experience, any vague reference to the fact that I might be, just *maaaaaaybe*, a little exhausted from the overall experience of being thrust into new motherhood, was met with a well-meaning *"Enjoy it now! She'll be grown up before you know it!"* or *"The days are long but the years are short"* *wink*, or *"Motherhood is such a blessing! Enjoy every minute!"* OR…*"Aren't you sleeping when the baby sleeps? That's the key to never struggling ever again at parenting, you know. Duh."* Any time I considered sharing an anecdote that dared to be any less than a 5 star review of motherhood, it was not accepted with the same open-armed reception that I'd get if I just gritted my teeth and said "Oh, everything's great! Thanks for asking!" I guess it was easier to lie and avoid having to explain and justify myself.

Was it because it made people uncomfortable to talk about something difficult, the same way they might shy away from hearing a piece of bad news? Was it because they just didn't have the time or energy to get down and dirty with "real-talk" as they were passing me on the way to the gym daycare? Was it because they refused to admit that they, too, were having a hard time parenting and that shoving their real feelings down was easier than admitting struggle? I don't know. I don't know the answers to these things, but what I *do* know is that I'm not the only one who has (not *had*, has, present tense, to be clear) hard, challenging, difficult, irritating, frustrating, and cry-inducing experiences while mothering, just like I have *hard*, challenging, difficult, irritating, frustrating and cry-inducing experiences IN MANY OTHER AREAS OF MY LIFE. Of this, I am certain. This book is filled with twenty-five examples of living evidence that I am not the only one. The purpose of this book is to allow you to see that you're not the only one, either.

Everything in life has a flip side. It goes without saying that any long-term experience you have in life is likely to have a few ups and downs along the way; sometimes they're quick and resolve easily, and other times they're more like phases of discomfort that are tricky to navigate. For some reason, there's a fear of sharing anything on the "down" side of parenting. Don't misread me: I love my child, and I am grateful for her every single day. We have incredibly beautiful moments together. She has 100% changed our lives for the better. She teaches me to do better every single day. She challenges me in good ways, too. My daughter, my partner, and myself are without a doubt the most important priorities in my life. I would do anything for them both and I wouldn't trade motherhood for the world. Hey, I know this is the way you feel too, so don't worry. I also know that as an emotionally-charged human you probably feel it's necessary to share this classic disclaimer to precede any complaining, too. Am I right? For what it's worth, acknowledging that you are having a difficult time and then admitting that parenting is hard does not discredit the amount of love you have for your child(ren). One does not cancel out the other. It's okay to admit that some days are hard. We're conditioned to believe that if we complain about parenting the sub-text is that we're blanketing the entire experience as bad. That's not the case, and that's what this book is here to support (Just so we're clear). The thing is...the positive, grateful-tinged experience is not the *only* experience, and that's not something only *you* are experiencing. It's *normal.* In the same way that we don't experience a perpetual state of sunlight, summer, or a full (hot) cup of coffee, everything in life has contrast.

We're here to dismantle the misconception that everything in the experience of motherhood is sunshine and rainbows. We're here to be raw and vulnerable about how there are many experiences and phases of motherhood, and not all of them are perfect. In fact, even the "perfect" ones have a good, healthy dose of difficulty. You are not a bad parent for admitting that your experience has hard, ugly pieces among the beauty. We are not blaming ourselves, our children, our partners, our parents, or anybody else for this experience, just like we wouldn't blame the world for throwing us a rainy day. Contrast is normal, healthy, beautiful, and necessary. Contrast helps us appreciate the flip side. Contrast allows us to see the stars more clearly through the darkness, the rainbow after the rain, and the harvest after the planting.

Momming Hard was written for you, dear mother, so you know that you're not alone. Momming is hard. As you'll see throughout this book...Momming a newborn is hard. Momming a toddler is hard. Momming a kindergartner is hard. Momming a school-aged kiddo is hard. Momming a teenager is hard. Momming a young adult is hard. Momming a new parent is hard. Momming an adoptive child is hard. Single momming is hard. Momming step-children is hard. Momming a child with special needs is hard. Momming while co-parenting is hard. Even the process of becoming a mom in the first place can be hard. Every stage has its challenges among the beauty. Nobody here is downplaying their love of their child(ren) in lieu of normalizing the conversation around the hard parts.

You're safe here. You're safe to admit some days are harder than others. You're safe to say it out loud: *this sh*t is hard.* The incredible women featured in these pages have bravely spoken up about their experiences, and though they absolutely, positively love their children beyond measure, sharing their stories serves as a reminder to us all — momming is hard, and it's okay to embrace the contrast. One story at a time, we're on a collective mission to normalize this conversation.

One day, when asked by a well-meaning acquaintance how she's doing on the way to the gym daycare, I hope a woman can honestly say: *"You know what, today has been hard. Today is not a good day. I'm looking forward to tomorrow when we can try again,"* and the person on the receiving end doesn't try to downplay her truth or counter her honesty with rose-coloured lenses, but just says simply: *"Yeah. Motherhood is hard sometimes. I've been there. Don't sweat it."*

We're all in this together. When you feel emotionally connected, inspired, or empathetic toward any of the authors in this book, I encourage you to reach out to the author(s) you resonate with and connect beyond the words on these pages. As women, mothers, and humans, we crave connection, and at the time of this publication[1], we're so starved and deprived of actual real-life connections with our fellow sisters — the women of our parenting communities. Reach out, thank them for their honesty, and connect on common ground. That's what collaborative books are for.

I hope you feel seen by reading this book. Don't forget to share your support for this project by showing off your copy on social media. These authors deserve all the credit for sharing their voices, and we hope that you have as much fun reading as we did creating.

Courtney St Croix

CEO, Leadher Publishing |Lead-her.com
@leadher_inc @leadherpublishing

[1] *Written February 2021, in the midst of a global pandemic.*

CHAPTER 1

Laura McLeod

FIND LAURA: **@LAMMLIFE _ XOXO**

Have you ever had a moment where the whole world stops, just like in the movies?

"He seems floppy."

These three words made my world come to a standstill. It is hard to explain a moment that logically does not make sense. Of course time did not stop, and the whole world did not freeze in place like a bad 80s sitcom, but that is exactly how I remember it. It was an out-of-body experience where everything around me paused, but my mind went into overdrive. I was frantically connecting seemingly insignificant moments together to try and make sense of what I had just been told:

"Your baby has Down syndrome."

At 27 years old I assumed I was untouchable. Up until this very moment I had lived comfortably, oblivious to the hardships that life likes to offer up. It is safe to say that was the day that I said good-bye to my carefree existence and was introduced to the heaviness of motherhood. Seemingly overnight my life had become scary, complicated, and unfamiliar. Nothing was fitting into the boxes they were supposed to. More than anything I remember the immediate weight that crept into my chest, my throat, and my shoulders — the invisible weight of a responsibility that I never wanted. There was no relief from the crushing pressure that had settled in. I was trapped in a hospital room — but worse — I was trapped in my own head.

My name is Laura, and I am the proud mom to my eight-year-old, Myles, and my six- year-old, Max. Myles has a dual diagnosis of Down syndrome and Autism. In the hospital the doctors suspected Myles had Down syndrome and it was confirmed by a blood test a week after he was born. We received his Autism diagnosis when he was 3 years old.

Our little family has come a long way. I do my best to juggle being a mom with my corporate career as a director for a software company. Myles and Max are both energetic, sweet boys who love to laugh and drive me crazy. We have a good life that has seen bad days and hard seasons. Navigating motherhood for a child with special needs has been, in a word, messy. Some days our mess feels perfect, and other days our mess breaks my heart. To be honest, it is a rollercoaster that I never wanted to get on, but now that I am here, I can say that we are finding our way.

When I left the hospital with Myles, I made the decision that there was no room for grief and sadness. I was his mother and I had to prove to the world that he was exactly who he was supposed to be.

What I did not realize at the time was that who I was really trying to convince was myself. Being Myles' mom has been a journey of self-discovery and brutal self-realization. He has exposed so many things about me that have been difficult to confront, and as each year passes he forces me to do better.

Myles' first year was pure joy. He was a dream baby — sleeping through the night, and, to everyone's amazement, meeting his physical milestones at the same time as a typically-developing child. Looking back on that first year, I know that I was completely genuine with my efforts; I was happy and confident that we could successfully navigate life with Myles. I suppose — like most things — it did not turn out to be that simple.

Although Myles continued to make strides with his physical development, it was becoming increasingly clear that his cognitive development was regressing, and we were seeing behaviours that did not fit with a Down syndrome diagnosis. The heaviness that I thought I had released was back — and this time the weight was more than I could bear. Our paediatrician confirmed what I had known in my heart: in addition to Down syndrome, Myles was also diagnosed with Autism. I had created a nice little picture of what life with Myles would be like, and Autism was not a part of that picture. That diagnosis confirmed that our family would never look how I had imagined, and I was absolutely gutted.

Unlike his Down syndrome diagnosis, I was not able to shake the heaviness I felt in my heart. I lost a dream that day — a dream that I had clung to for three years, and letting go was unimaginable. I could not dare admit to anyone the sadness that now inhabited every part of me. I didn't want to burden anyone with my grief, but most of all, I didn't want anyone to pity us. I remember going into overdrive coming up with how to spin his diagnosis like I was a PR firm covering up a celebrity scandal. What I was really doing was overcompensating. If I could convince everyone else that our new diagnosis was fine then maybe no one would see the truth. Part of me wished so badly that someone would see through me; that someone would call me out so that I would have to come clean. The truth was...I was angry; I was exhausted; I was a total wreck. I did not know what to do with all these emotions. I was so ashamed of my thoughts and feelings that I had to bury them.

Do you ever play the "at least" game? You know, the one where you think up all of the reasons why your circumstances are not as bad as someone else's? When we were navigating Myles' Down syndrome diagnosis I would always tell myself, "at least he doesn't have Autism." Except...what happens when your "at least" becomes your reality? I understood exactly what it felt like to know that your child's diagnosis was another mother's biggest fear. Every single day pregnant women around the world are tested to find out if they are carrying a child with Down syndrome, and many choose not to continue with that pregnancy. It's a crushing feeling to think that there are people praying not to have your life. Ironically, however, I had been doing the same thing all along. Admitting that Autism was my greatest fear felt like a huge betrayal to Myles and to everyone in the Autism community. I couldn't dare share these feelings with anyone; I had a horrible secret and the only way I could ensure that no one would ever know the truth was to pretend that everything was okay.

It started small by just keeping my struggles and feelings private, but over time I entered what I like to call my "fake positivity phase." The positivity that I was spewing became my ticket to acceptance. The narrative that I had created was as good as a made-for-TV movie — a happy couple accepts, loves, and advocates for their special needs child. I became an expert at knowing exactly what people wanted to hear. If I met someone for the first time and the topic of kids came up, I would drop the special needs bomb and feel their discomfort followed by my own. I would quickly continue with how well Myles was doing and how much joy he has brought to our lives.

I could see the relief come over their face, and the awkwardness in the room would disappear. I quickly learned that people only like linear stories with a happy ending. The messy, up and down, roller coaster life we had was not digestible. It made people uncomfortable — so I never told it.

In this fake positivity world, I had a few rules that I religiously obeyed:

1. Always ignore your true feelings. Bury them deep down where they can never be discovered.

2. Constantly come up with ways that your situation could be worse in order to guilt yourself into being grateful for your life.

3. Obsessively try and control outcomes so you can keep up with your image.

4. Never acknowledge your struggle so that you can continue to ignore your reality.

I really did get caught up in what I thought our life should look like. These rules helped me hide, but they also prevented me from really *seeing* my son. What I focused on instead was everything that he wasn't. I started to resent other families who seemingly had it much easier than I did. I would romanticize about what life would be like if Myles didn't have Autism, and I ended up spending most of my time in my own head.

I withdrew from many social activities because I found it difficult to connect with anyone. When we were with families who did not have a child with special needs it was impossible for them to relate, and the fear of judgement and rejection kept me from opening up about our life and experiences. In the special needs community, it was too complicated to be honest. In a world of advocacy and inclusion how do you admit that you wish your child was "normal?" In my close circle of friends and family I would have the occasional breakdown, but overall I did not want anyone to worry about me. Most of all, I did not want to admit that I felt like a failure. I could not fix this; I could not make it better, and I was a fraud. I could be surrounded by family and friends, but always alone with my feelings. When no one truly sees you, it is extremely isolating.

Despite feeling lonely I probably could have kept up this facade for-ever, but as always Myles had his own plans. See, it can be difficult to keep up appearances when you do not have a willing participant in your charade. I started to understand that the world is inclusive to people with special needs if they fit into a certain box. When I found out Myles had Down syndrome I immediately started googling and was presented with thousands of images of people with Down syndrome who were absolutely thriving. They were running busi-nesses, winning medals, graduating university, and driving cars. I welcomed and accepted this life for Myles, as did the world wide web. What I did not find in my search was a nonverbal 8-year-old in diapers exhibiting multiple sensory-inducing behaviours like hum-ming, rocking, and tapping. I knew my son made people uncom-fortable. What I did not know was that their discomfort would make me uncomfortable. In those moments the image I had been working so hard to create began to crack, finally crashing down completely when Myles had a public outburst that I was unable to contain. I can still feel the burn that only comes from utter shame and embarrass-ment. It was on display for the world to see that my son was out of control and I was powerless to manage the situation. Looking back, I believe this was Myles' way of standing his ground and saying: "Enough already, Mom!"

That day was the catalyst for significant change. I had spent the bet-ter part of four years putting on a show, convincing everyone that I was a special needs super mom. I had built this narrative around our family like a security blanket that kept me ignorant to the truth about what was really going on. That day I had to face a hard reality about my relationship with Myles, and it was time to make some big adjustments.

In most relationships, when things get hard you can choose to love or you can choose to leave, but what happens when that relationship is with your child? As a mother I had assumed my love for Myles was a given, but turns out…it's not. To truly love when the going gets tough is a choice, and a choice I was not making. I was so fixated on failed expectations and resentment that I lost sight of what was most important. I was clinging to a superficial image that I was desperately trying to achieve. It was at this time that I stopped choosing to see Myles from a lens of unconditional love. I wasn't strong enough to put Myles first and tune out the rest of the world. I got upset when he would shout and scream at the park and the other kids and parents would stare. I would be embarrassed when he would act out and cause a scene. I would get angry when he would hit or pinch. I always believed that a mother's love was simple and pure, but I was realizing it was much more complicated than that. I started to question if it was possible and normal to fall in and out of love with your child.

After many sleepless nights and internal battles, I decided to think of unconditional love not as a given, but as an active choice. That was the day that my relationship with Myles took on a new life. Suddenly the shouting was Myles' way to tell everyone he was excited, acting out meant he needed attention, and when he would hit and pinch I could see that he was expressing his frustrations. Not only did the active choice to love unconditionally help me understand the meaning behind his negative behaviours, but it also opened my eyes to all of the amazing things Myles was accomplishing. I had failed to notice his progress because my focus was solely on the outcome looking exactly as I had pictured.

Hearing your child say the words "I love you" is a moment that all parents wait for and dream about. Myles is nonverbal and so not hearing those three little words come from his mouth was a big source of sadness and disappointment for me. When I started to lead with love instead of expectations, I was able to notice things that I never had before. Myles tells me he loves me in his own way a million times a day! He has a special smile just for me, and knows the exact time I need a kiss to cheer me up. He also gives me the biggest bear hugs that leave me with no doubt that this boy loves me to his very core.

The consequence of choosing unconditional love is that it forces you to drop all expectations. If there are no conditions then there cannot be any expectations — it's that simple. Can you have hopes and dreams for your child? Of course, but what I have come to learn is that they need to stay at a macro level. My hope for Myles has always been for him to be happy, but somewhere along the way that macro goal turned into very specific outcomes based on an image of happiness that I had created, and when those outcomes weren't achieved I gave us both a failing grade. I was in a constant cycle of build up, let down, and resentment. Halloween is a perfect example. Each year I would search for the perfect costume and build up to the big day, then be disappointed when Myles did not want to carve pumpkins or trick-or-treat.

Every Halloween I would end the night in tears, resenting the fact that I was robbed of moments with my child that seem so normal for everyone else. This Halloween it was time to put all the self-reflection that I had been doing into practise. When I really thought about it on a macro level, my goal was for Myles to have a great Halloween. Period. Full stop. Mother Nature was on my side, and it was a beautiful fall day. Just before lunch Myles found his Superman costume, brought it to me, and signaled that he wanted to put it on. Old me would have refused his request; It was too early in the day, his costume could get dirty, and this just isn't how it works! Consciously choosing love instead, I got him into his costume and we went outside to enjoy the beautiful day. He ran, skipped and played Superman; it was a joy to watch. Later that evening when it was time to trick-or-treat, Myles did not want to put his costume back on, but he did seem eager to join his brother to go from house to house. I didn't force it. He went out in his plain clothes and had the best time ringing doorbells, getting candy, and practising the sign for thank you. Was this the Instagram-worthy Halloween that I had pictured? No, but we did achieve the goal: Myles had a great Halloween, and for the first time I didn't end the night in tears.

I had spent a lot of years building a giant wall of positivity in an effort to avoid grief, trauma, and my unresolved emotions. Trying to hold it all together with a smile on my face was draining, and Myles' public outburst pushed me to surrender. I found myself ready to admit that everything was not fine. My life was hard and messy, and I was terrified that I was not strong enough to be the mother Myles needed. Once I acknowledged these beliefs, the weight that I had been carrying for years lifted. As cliché as it sounds, I really felt like I was set free. I thought that if I took away the facade that I had built our lives on, our whole world would crumble. And you know what? Maybe it did, but maybe that was exactly what we needed. Now I could rebuild. I looked at it like a fresh start, and this time I would be a little braver, a little wiser, and a little kinder to myself.

As I began to rebuild my relationship with Myles and shed years of guilt and shame around not being enough, it was high time for a new set of rules.

In my new, authentic, and honest world, I religiously obey the following rules:

1. Always face your emotions head on.

2. Never subscribe to fake positivity, as it will only invalidate your circumstances and limit your growth.

3. Constantly remember that other people's comfort is not

your responsibility. They will either grow with you or you will leave them behind.

4. Obsessively surrender control and acknowledge that forcing and manipulating outcomes does not guarantee success and happiness.

I wish I could put a bow on this and give you the happy ending that comes with any feel good story; but if you recall, your comfort is not my responsibility. ;) There is no happily ever after in this story because this isn't the end. Right now we are in a good season, we've found a rhythm, but eventually we will fall out of sync and have to go back to the drawing board. As Myles develops we will have more to celebrate, but also more to navigate. It's time to get comfortable living in the grey area and trusting that no matter how messy it gets, we will always find our way.

CHAPTER 2

SHARANA ALI

FIND SHARANA: **@BOSSTHESIXEDITION**

As a mom, you're stuck in this weird world of extremes— particularly when you hear or see other moms doing their thing. You only see or hear about "masters" or "disasters."

In some circles, motherhood is described as this blissful experience filled with only laughter and moments of magic. It's this sequin-filled time where you poop rainbows and have butterflies fluttering around you. This is the version of motherhood that I grew up knowing and seeing. It was the assumption that moms somehow know it all — and do it all — with a smile on their face, and everyone lives happily ever after. The End.

Alternatively, and more recently (thankfully!), there has been a spotlight on motherhood as a Groundhog Day in hell filled with yelling, temper tantrums, sleepless nights, a kid who won't eat anything, and a boatload of dishes, where all the pressure is on one person in the home — YOU. It's filled with guilt, shame, and anxiety. All you want to do is hide in your bathtub with a glass of red wine until your child turns nineteen.

But, how? How could motherhood be either/or? What about both? And what if it is both versions, within minutes? What if both descriptions are okay, so long as you as a human are mentally, physically, and emotionally okay?

What if momming is hard as shit — and also easy, magical, and heartbreaking? What if we accept and celebrate it all, instead of boxing moms into a dichotomy, or telling moms how they're *supposed* to feel?

I'm Sharana Ali — a sarcastic single mom, the badass business owner of BOSS The Six Edition, a full-time Ontario government employee, and a 9:00 dark roast coffee drinker, followed by a glass of red at 5:00. And, I am on a mission of world domination.

While I work to wrap all of those descriptors up into a beautiful bow, I'm a 30-something-year-old human just living one day at a time, in hopes of raising a whole, compassionate, strong-minded child — who will one day dominate her own world.

For me, THIS SHIT IS HARD, but it has also been rewarding, educating, and life-altering. That pretty bow I was talking about earlier? This life is honestly not something I would trade for anything.

No one prepared me for any of this. None of the emotions, none of the shitty thoughts that run through my mind. No one says, *"Hey! You're going to love that little human with every fiber of your body as much as you probably will want to run away, quit everything, and join the circus."*

But I do it, despite the lack of preparation.

I do it because, like most things in life, the hardest shit brings the greatest sense of joy and accomplishment — and being a single mom brings with it a new layer of HARD.

I didn't expect to do it alone. I never wanted to.

I always knew that I wanted to be a mom, but I wanted it all — I wanted to be a mom the way society at the time defined what a "mom" was. I wanted the happy home, the loving husband, the home-cooked meals, the white picket fence, and warm cookies from the oven.

My "la-la land" dream wasn't of me being a single mom living with my parents, where every decision concerning the wellbeing of this human fell in my lap, while simultaneously trying to deal with society, the internet, and grandparents having an opinion on anything and everything.

I planned to tag team this shit, but not with the world — with one other person! All that to say: when I tried it failed miserably, and so now single motherhood is my jam.

I'm a proud single mama, but holy hell does it come with some baggage. Co-parenting, living in a multi-generational home where there is no such thing as a "break" (even if my kid isn't physically with me 24/7)...it makes for quite the journey.

Here's the *fun* part of being a single mom and a co-parenting partner (note the sarcasm when I say "fun"): While on one hand you can parent on your own terms, on the other hand, you may not always agree with decisions that need to be made together — or with how the other parent has decided to handle something. But you still need to present a united front, or those little geniuses will get the better of you — both of you. Making the decision to go our separate ways was the right one for us, but it comes with its own set of challenges.

For many reasons, I was excited by the fact that I was going to be a single mom (scared shitless of course, but excited).

Finally, I could be the mom I always wanted to be without someone saying or thinking that I'm a quack for mothering non-traditionally. I thought that this would be my opportunity to completely raise my daughter to be the person I envisioned her being, embracing her emotional health, letting her pave her own path, and giving her the liberty and confidence to make her own decisions — at any age. Apparently this way of mothering was a big no-no, because God forbid she trusted herself at two years old (yes, there's a ton of sarcasm and passive aggressiveness there).

It turns out that I *am* parenting, as some call it, "non-traditionally." My daughter calls a lot of the shots in her life with two rules in mind: no hurting yourself or those around you, and know that every decision made creates an impact, whether negative or positive. With all of this said, though, there is another parent involved in this girl's life. One who doesn't parent the way that I do, and never will. I had to grow to accept and respect that, while also maintaining some of the rules and expectations placed on my kid while she wasn't with me!

Imagine having to raise a human with someone you personally couldn't *live* with?...*That's fucked up!* That's not the way that we planned on things going when we committed to a relationship, assuming it meant "forever." But, that's exactly what I'm doing. We are equal parenting partners with the single goal of raising what we hope to be a happy human. While my daughter is with me, I parent the way I see fit; and when she's not with me, her other parent does their thing to the best of their ability. Does that cause confusion, and sometimes pint-sized manipulation from someone who reaches just above my hip? YES!

And so, despite not actually being together, we have to be united.

I would argue that we actually have to have greater communication than when we were married! This means conversations about her day-to-day, making decisions together about the larger aspects of her life, and keeping each other informed as much as possible. Personally, as a mom, this challenged SO MANY FREAKING BOUNDARIES. The concept of continuing conversations with her other parent was anxiety-inducing, but required me to really refocus my energy onto my daughter — fast and furiously — because if I didn't have the conversations with him, I would be taken for a ride by the mini monster...like the gummy bear incident.

The gummy bear incident. My daughter was potty training and told me that every time she went potty at Dad's house, she would get a gummy bear — whether she actually 'went' or not. I thought, okay, if it incentivises her to go — let's do it. My darling daughter racked up 10 gorgeous mini gummies until I realized that something seemed a little fishy. A quick call to her dad, and it turns out...no dice. He actually wasn't rewarding her for using the potty, just trying to get her into a routine of going when she felt like she had to go...which is what I was doing all along.

I laugh about it now, but damn, she's good — and I'm so freaking trusting! While there was no harm nor foul in the consumption of gummies, it did make me realize that even the slightest of parenting needed us to work together and be a team, despite what our parenting dynamic looked like. So, even if I was a single mom — doing it all while she was with me, making all of the primary decisions — in her larger world, there would always be two parents, and whether physically together or not, we needed to present ourselves (to some extent) as *one.*

I always say that being a single mom allowed me to be the mom that I wanted to be. I do get to make up the rules as I go along. I get to impart the wisdom that I want my kid to have, and while it often feels like a HUGE responsibility doing it on my own, I'm pretty lucky to be living with my parents — for their extra eyes and arms to jump in on a whim.

But, like a lot of motherhood experiences, it's not all a bed of roses. Imagine being a mom and doing your mom thing, while also being a daughter with your mom continuing to mother you while being a grandmother! It is as confusing as it sounds.

Living in a multi-generational home is tricky! It's messy. It's my biggest blessing but can also be such a curse. I have the luxury of extra hands when I need to take a shower, and extra eyes to make sure that my daughter isn't literally crawling up the wall. I have the support of cooking together, a warm tidy house that we built together, and the occasional sleepovers at Grandma and Grandpa's being just down the hall. But, that sounds like a bed of roses...and therefore wouldn't belong in this book.

When it comes to the tougher decisions, sometimes the lines get blurred, and the water is as muddy as it gets. Mothering in a way that I see fit, in alignment with my ideas and expectations, in a generation that is far from the generation I grew up in — it's hard! Sometimes it's uncomfortable to say, *"Hey, wait...I'm the mom!"* without sounding like an ungrateful brat. It's a fine balance between honouring my role as a mom and their roles as grandma and grandpa or uncle. I don't want to step on toes, but I also don't want someone else raising my child when she is with me.

And so, my best option is to carefully pick my battles. I let them take their roles seriously. I let them spoil, and break some of the rules (as few as I have). I let them guide, support, and celebrate. But, when it comes down to it, we've had to have some incredibly tough conversations in which I admit that I love, respect, and appreciate them to death, but for the life of me — I also want the opportunity to be a mom, and sometimes that means that I need them to bite their tongues or not give in to her every desire.

Being a mother who prides herself on extremely open communication with her child means that the conversations we have already extend far beyond many of the conversations I've ever had with my parents, even at my current age. Already, my daughter and I have spoken of the human body (with accurate language), terrorism, social injustices, racsim, systemic racism, sex, sexuality, breaking gender norms, the power of choice, and the importance of standing true to her choices and opinions despite what anyone may say.

Many argue that it's too much for a four-year-old, that it takes away her innocence and imagination. Ultimately, I argue that I want her to be informed, to arm her with the truth of knowing that she always has permission to ask questions, and to feel as though she can come to me to talk about anything without a sense of embarrassment or shame. As I know more, I teach more; as I learn, we grow together.

Is it the right way? I have no idea. What's the *right* way to do things, anyway? Do any of us moms know if anything we are doing is right or wrong? We know this shit is hard, and it's easy, and it's loving, and it's heartbreaking. Where this sort of mothering comes from for me is that I wish I was better informed as I grew up. The real world shocked me, often and continuously. I just want to prepare her more.

Seeing before me two strong parents who continue to inspire me also comes with a heightened sense of mom guilt. I can't do it like them. And while I know I don't want to — nor do I have to — I often feel like I'm tipping the scales against the wellbeing of my child because I'm going against generational norms. Thoughts that I'm royally fucking up because I often don't know what I'm doing — while also knowing that I don't want to make the same mistakes that my parents made — creep up more often than I would like to admit.

Would I have the same thoughts if I actually lived alone? I don't know. But, truthfully, could I be the type of mom that I am today — with the ability to genuinely spend time with my daughter as opposed to upkeep a house — without them? I don't know.

The whole multigenerational home thing...it's a challenge. I cry often. I laugh more. But I also get to witness my daughter growing up with her grandparents. I get to see the bond and connection between the past generation and future, daily. It truly is a beautiful disaster that I proudly call my life.

This life...it isn't for the faint of heart. In fact, it takes more emotion, grit, and courage than anything I've ever done in my life. I've only wanted to quit every single day, and yet I keep going with the hope and the promise that tomorrow will be a little brighter. That's the thing with moms — we do it for the toothy grins, loud laughs, big hugs, and whispers of "I love you." It makes it all worth it. Especially being a single mom, it's these moments of my WHY that get me through the days and hours when we are apart.

I remember speaking with a good friend, and she told me that she could do with a day or two without her little one. I knew what she meant: she wanted a breather. She wanted a moment to herself to just *be*. I know we all say it every once in a while, but when it becomes your reality, it makes you think twice.

That's not to say that we can't wish for a sweet escape, or desire some time alone. I think both are extremely healthy when you're a woman, no less a mom. But I think it's safe to say that even in those moments of solitude you often end up thinking of the little monsters. How many of us, post bedtime, jump onto our phones only to scroll through past pictures or videos of our little ones? I do it all the time. Or, at a night out with our friends ends with talking up a storm about the latest and greatest thing your child is doing? Me too, me too. I see you.

There's no "off" switch when you're a mom. The emotions, worry, and love don't just stop when your kids aren't with you physically. In fact, it all just heightens — there IS no break — there's no "time out" or "night off" — even if you're a single mom.

I'll never forget the first night that I was away from my daughter. I had only been broken up with her dad for a couple of days. She had never spent a moment away from me, with the exception of daycare, let alone a night away. In the days preceding, I made a list of everything I wanted to do to occupy my time. I wanted to look at the time away as a chance to dedicate some time to myself — to "un-mom" — if that makes sense. The list included: going to bed early, drinking a glass of wine, taking a bubble bath, and watching lots of Netflix. Essentially, I wanted to flood myself with things to do — things that I loved to do — prior to being a mom. I also wanted to be sure that I could blur out any difficult feelings that might come from the awareness of being alone.

Nothing from that list happened. I sobbed the entire time and was consumed by mom guilt until my eyes burned and I drifted off to sleep. As much as I truly craved a "night off," it was so far from the glitzy night that I hoped for. None of my time away from my daughter ever is. Sure, now it's a little easier, but I still miss her dearly, talk about her non-stop, and count down the hours and minutes until she returns.

These are the moments in motherhood that confuse me the most. The paradoxes. All of them. On one hand, YES — like so many of you reading this book, a night out on the town reminiscent of life pre-kids sounded like a dream. But when I got "the time," I hated it. The fact of the matter is, I also have quickly come to terms with the fact that there's no going back in so many ways, and I don't want to. For the most part, I'm no longer that girl. My life is no longer as carefree, and as crazy as it sounds, I don't hate it. Even in the shittiest of moments, I don't hate it — I just don't *love* it.

Motherhood is, in fact, paradoxical. It's everything — all emotions, thoughts, and actions all at the same time — even if none of it makes sense. It's not knowing how you will get through the day, yet still missing yesterday. It is hard. It is beautiful. It is exactly what you define it to be.

This is MY motherhood. It's unlike anyone else's, and that's why this shit is so hard. There's no manual or one-hat-fits-all. It's literally throwing the dice to what you feel fits and hoping for the best. But, from one mom to another, as long as you are confident in your decisions (and mama, BE CONFIDENT in them), you are doing a damn good job.

CHAPTER 3

SHAUNA CLARK

FIND SHAUNA: **@SLARK.10**

Shauna is a teacher who lives with her husband, Nic, and three boys, ages 6, 4, and 1, on the shores of Lake Huron in Goderich, Ontario. She is expecting her fourth child in June 2021.

If I make spaghetti for dinner, I know I need to make a full box. We need a full box because, firstly, we are a family of five. I know I want leftovers for my lunch as well as for my two school-aged boys, and my husband tends to fast until 5:30 each day, so he's super hungry by the time dinner rolls around. Super interesting information, eh? No, not at all...but this is important information that takes up room in my brain, and — believe it or not — knowing this information makes my life easier.

After the birth of my third son, I struggled greatly with the decision to return to work full-time or take a break from teaching to be home with my kids. There were undoubtedly pros and cons to each side, and I realize the privilege that I have to even have the option. In the end, the gig that I prefer is the one outside of the house — not just "prefer," but feels like part of my identity and brings me immense joy. I can't imagine being anything other than a teacher.

When I was on maternity leave with my last little, I remember a friend posting something on Facebook about solutions to staying on top of laundry. Staying on *top?* I did laundry every day. I dominated my laundry, not just "stayed on top." I would wash, dry, and put away all in the same day. Who were these people that did not complete this method? Agents of chaos? Slaves to disorganization or dwellers of laundry piles? Not me.

Well, let's just fast forward a year in the role of sole laundry person for a family of five who is not home during the day. It seemed my status as Champion Laundry Gal had shifted slightly.

Let the washing machine cycle twice with the same load? Yep!

Leave laundry in the dryer for multiple days? Check!

Let it pile up, unfolded, to the point that I may have lost a child for a brief three minutes? You got it!

By working outside of the house full-time, I let a lot of things (RE: housekeeping things) slide. I don't love this. In fact, it causes me even more stress and anxiety. But of all of the things to juggle in terms of returning to work full-time while being a mom, the hardest thing is knowing that I need to use an entire box of spaghetti in order to feed my family dinner tonight and have enough for lunch the next day.

And no, it's not actually the act of doing the shopping or making the dinner that induces stress; it's the full box, the mental load, the invisible load. This burden of knowledge is hard for me to balance as a working mother.

Before you think that I must be married to an absentee partner, nothing could be further from the truth. I married a man with a plan (and even more sexy, the drive to achieve that plan). When I first met Nic, he freely (but not as confidently) came out as a workaholic. He had a plan that included financial freedom within his lifetime, and he had been working at it for years prior to meeting me. His work is as much a part of his identity as teaching is to mine. To this day, he is exactly the guy I first met 11 years ago, and I have watched him become a supportive husband and an amazing dad of four. But he has one additional child that isn't a human: his contracting business. It is his fifth child that allows our family to enjoy the lifestyle that we have.

Now, in order to accommodate our shared professional addictions, we do have some fairly straight-up divisions of labour in our home which help us to maintain the illusion of "normal:"

I do not typically do garbage, but have been known to set gag-worthy collections on the front step, much closer to the physical garbage container than previously located.

He's likely never gotten a stain out of one of the boys' shirts, but he will do laundry if he risks leaving the house naked.

Whoever is home first makes dinner. Shocker. That's usually me. We have designated jobs for after 5:30:

I clean dishes.

He cleans floors, counters, the table, and children.

We put our kids to bed together (unless I am in the first trimester of pregnancy, and then I go to bed before anyone else).

The point of this is that we share the physical load. Not completely

50/50, but it swings and adapts on a daily basis in order to support each other as parents, professionals, and partners.

But we cannot, no matter what, share the mental load. Nic cannot unburden my spaghetti traumas, and that sucks.

Is it that we can't share the mental load because I won't give it up? Or is it because there's just no way for Nic to live inside of my brain, and no logical way to communicate the *Beautiful* Mind room of daily, monthly, and seasonal minutiae, without feeling like a lunatic? Either point is valid, but I feel like all women, as soon as we become moms, start amassing an even larger, more complex, and perilously stacked mental load. Somehow we can balance when essential baby wellness checks need to happen, the perpetual Diaper Situation™, track when the baby is about to burst out of size 6 month clothing, maintain an ongoing inventory of deep freezers and pantries, keep track of each child's (and husband's) toys/clothing/phone/keys/etc., and manage the ever-changing invite list to child number 1's upcoming birthday party — all while tracking our peak ovulation days. The things we lend our mental capacity to just continue to morph and grow and get heavier as our children grow up and/or we add more to the mix.

So what is the mental load? Well, let's think about Christmas morning, because it's fresh in my mind. I planned gifts for the teachers at daycare and school, the bus driver, the children Nic and I share, the children in my class, and our immediate families. I made the lists of everything we needed to have in the house to ensure Santa had milk, cookies, and reindeer food, as well as all of the wrap, tape, tags, bows for gifts, all the necessary food for Christmas morning breakfast and Christmas day dinner, plus all the "other stuff" which might come in handy if visitors stop by or a last minute invite pops up. Now, these lists don't reflect the physical act and time of completing these tasks, but these lists are the physical sliver of the mental load that is crucial in executing Christmas.

It's the planning that goes into making sure a household runs smoothly — knowing where the hats, mittens, and snow pants are so that you can get out the door easily in the morning. It is also the reason the phrase, *"Mom, where is my ____?"* exists. Add to that the physical stress of doing these activities and raising children, and eventually there is going to be a system overload (aka: meltdown).

Let's take a little trip back to March 2020. Being on maternity leave, we took a one-week family vacation for the week before March Break. I was sitting poolside in Punta Cana when Nic alerted me that the NBA had shut down due to COVID-19. This was Wednesday, and by Friday afternoon, we had learned about schools being closed for an extra two weeks and the province-wide lockdown. Despite the panic and gut-stewing process that was getting my family home via international airports and airborne petri tubes, this worldwide emergency would serve as an additional wheelbarrow for my over-packed mental load. I recognize and respect how absolutely hard and emotionally draining this seasonal lockdown cycle is on many, many families, but for the first time in our married life, during the first lockdown, Nic was home…A LOT.

Due to having to quarantine if you'd been out of the country, Nic couldn't run his business upon our return — and quite frankly, everything was scary at the time, to the extreme that I was Lysoling and disinfecting our cereal boxes and letting them sit for 3 days. Needless to say, he didn't feel it was safe for him or his employees to return to work. You know what this meant for me? HELP! For the first time in our parenting experiment, there was someone else in the house who knew we were down to three granola bars because he was making snacks and dinner just as often as me. Not long after, the kids started calling for Mom or Dad evenly! Nic being home meant that I had a lot of time for me — time that I have never really had as a mother. I began running a 5K each day. I had time alone in my house while he took the boys on hikes. I didn't have the demands of my teaching job and, honestly, my mental health was stellar despite not being able to see any of our support system. I still shouldered more of the mental load, but his assistance with the physical load and childrearing made such a difference at the end of the day because there was still time — a lot of it — for me!

Fast-forward and we are now three weeks into our second lockdown. Has this heightened state of Corona-Nirvana only multiplied? Am I now running 10km a day and sending grocery lists telepathically to Nic? Uhhh, no. This time around, I am teaching Kindergarten full-time while my two sons, Grade 1 and JK, are also online. I thank my lucky stars that daycare is open and I don't have my youngest roaming around, because in this lockdown he might go missing for more than three minutes amidst the canyons of laundry. Nic walks out the door with him around 7:15 am and returns around 5:30 pm… and all that in-between stuff that has to happen? It's on me. I am in charge of everything. My resume has exploded in *Lockdown 2: The Sequel.* I am the full-time chef, maid, nurse, referee, mom, teacher (for my class and my sons), as well as chauffeur for when we need to pick the youngest up from daycare (because my mom guilt won't let me let him stay there all day despite the fact that I am so burnt out). Just when the mental load was tolerable for me, we added in three different timetables to juggle and no additional space, time, or people to manage them.

I keep telling myself that this is all short-term so I can forgo my run, that relaxing evening bath, my favourite Netflix series, or anything that brings me joy that's just for me. It's my mental load and I'm the only one who can shuffle the contents to make room for the necessities. However, what I've come to realize is that, for me, the mental load is only manageable when I take care of myself and my needs. It's like those little tasks that I'm so quick to sacrifice are the ones that help to create a more stable wheelbarrow to cart around this Herculean effort. When I've carved that time out for myself, I can complete the physical load fairly smoothly, and the hiccups don't set me off.

But when I'm pressed for time or utterly exhausted, who do I put last? Myself. Then, those hiccups make everything so heavy and burdening. All of the open tabs swirling around in my brain of what I need to do have made getting to the physical tasks absolutely impossible. By the time the end of the day rolls around, I don't want to look at a screen, call anyone to book an appointment, or take inventory of laundry. I am barely staying afloat. I know what I could do to make this slightly more tolerable for me, but I am so exhausted I just can't. I know I am not the only mother feeling this way right now, but I also know some of you are probably thinking, "Why the hell don't you get your husband to do those things?"

The answer is that I don't really know. Truthfully, I can't tell you why, but I do believe it's more my control issues rather than him not thinking to offer. For example, Nic is quite capable of calling and making a doctor's appointment. However, they'd name off a random day and time and he'd respond, "Sure. Let's book it." But it's my schedule that he needs to know, because I'd be the one taking the child. I know what day is my double prep day, when I have a staff or division meeting after work, what our childcare may be doing on certain days of the week, and when my one coveted hair appointment every 6 weeks is. Mental. Load. I would likely have to call, cancel, and rebook. In essence, it's easier if I just do it in the first place. Sound familiar?

I don't begrudge Nic for not knowing these meetings or appointments. I don't keep track of his appointments and meetings outside of family obligations, so why should he know mine? I do begrudge that he very rarely can take the children to said appointments. Were he to make the appointment with the intention of taking them himself, it would be his mental burden to sort out schedules (and a small waterfall of tasks off of my plate).

In many ways, it feels like his career is "more important" than mine. Despite our shared commitment to Workaholics Anonymous, our partnership tends to slink back into the sewage pipe which empties into the 1950s — and to be fair, this prioritization was systematically embedded in our marital set up. While we love taking time off of work with pay for the birth of a child, it isn't an option for a self-employed person. Being that my job had a paid leave, naturally I took the boys to every appointment when they were little and managed the household necessities that came with having a family. There's been stints of back-to-work and maternity leave woven into the last six years of our marriage. From the get-go of our relationship, placement insecurities on my board resulted in "my career" quickly becoming "my job." The perks of my Union became the pitfall of my career. That fraction of job security that I was afforded meant that it was easier for me to leave and harder and harder to balance the growing workload at home.

Here's our reality: Nic rarely leaves work early. If he's not working his employees aren't working, and that affects multiple people. He and his employees aren't on a salary, and I am. My deadlines are fairly scheduled within the year, but his are unpredictable. While money is an important factor in our division of labour, it's not just our personal finances that led to our divisions. It's keeping employees and customers happy, getting work completed in a timely manner, and staying on top of the massive amount of paperwork involved in running your own business. In my career, another capable, passionate, and dedicated human will step in in my absence and students will still learn.

Now, I could go on a long tirade that statistically mothers are carrying the mental load due to how our society is constructed, and how I believe this won't change until stereotypes aren't thrust upon us and paid parental leave is longer (or even an option) for both parents. I can share these discussions with my husband, sons, and girlfriends, but discussion doesn't change anything for me right now in this stage of motherhood. What I can do, for me, right now, is prioritize myself. When I prioritize myself, it means letting something else go...but it turns out that I don't actually care about that sacrificed obligation because I know I can get to it later, and mentally I feel so much lighter.

I love running. Now, I don't love the physical act while I am completing it, but I absolutely love what it does for my mind. I am not a fast or competitive runner. I even stopped tracking my time because I started obsessing about it when the real reason for my run was so that I didn't run away from my family. However, recently during weeks 7-13 of this pregnancy, I couldn't bring myself to do anything. I was feeling next-level exhaustion and nausea, and now, at my 20 week mark, I literally just can't seem to make the time for myself. In the absence of these runs, a new inner monologue takes its place:

"...It's not that I physically do not have the time, being home in a lockdown and all. I'd prefer to be outside, but our Canadian winter and my growing bump means no outdoor running because I am worried about a fall and I have some pretty severe sciatica happening...but that's not why I'm not doing it. The only ones using the treadmill right now are the littles, and I literally have no excuse for something that I know will make me feel 9 million times more able to tackle the world right now. Yet, at the same time, I have 9 million reasons why I can't seem to get up early and do it ..."

In the middle of this lockdown, in the moments that my sons are preoccupied or sleeping, I am completely consumed in the mental load (and the running monologue that accompanies it) and can't even get to "my share" of the physical load. I know this lockdown won't last, and I sincerely hope that some normalcy comes back soon. Nic does listen and tries to help (without me asking him). Yet, I know that if I were to get up and go for a run tomorrow morning, we would all have a much better day.

Now, there is a good chance that running isn't the thing that fills your cup, and that's totally okay. I have mama pals that are chronic cleaners, amazing bakers, book worms, and walkers. It doesn't matter WHAT it is...But are you DOING it?

I know I am better prepared to handle the mental load and execute the physical load if I make time for myself. I have more patience with my boys and am able to regulate my big feelings while dealing with theirs. I am not saying this will work for you, but when I chat with my girlfriends I see that if everyone can have their time to do "their thing" it makes us all feel like better mothers, and it is my hope that it will make you feel the same.

The decision fatigue, the neverending laundry and cleaning, the dinners — it's not going to go anywhere anytime soon. So, for your personal well being and mental health, trust me when I say that you need to find something to fill your cup.

How I do it is by waking up hours earlier than anyone else in my family. Waking up 2 hours before the rest of my home allows me to sit in quiet and lace up my beloved runners. It sets the whole tone for my day. The first week of waking up at that ungodly hour was not fun, but a small waterfall of good things started to happen. To get up that early meant that I had to stop scrolling my phone late at night and actually choose sleep instead. And because of the physical activity, I was falling asleep sooner with more restful sleep. More sleep made that ungodly hour seem slightly more manageable. Before I knew it, my body just became accustomed to it and a habit had formed.

It took a lot of trial and error to see where, when, and what this time for me would look like. I've been a mother for six years, and it's only in the last two that I would rate my mental health and wellbeing as "great." I did things that I enjoy, like acting in plays, following an exercise program, taking relaxing baths after the boys go to bed, squeezing a run in after supper and before bedtime, asking Nic to do things at home so that I could go out with girlfriends and not walk into a delayed punishment of a kitchen to clean when I got home. It never clicked until the woman who taught me how to run properly described how she woke up hours earlier than her four children to make time and space for herself. I tried it the very next day. Now, if you're in the depths of sleep deprivation, grief, or a lockdown, this perhaps isn't the time to find out what you need. You're in a place of survival that's very different from thriving, but if you think you're in a place where you can prioritize you, I want you to!

I do have hope that societal constructs will change. I already see it in the way that we are raising our sons and daughters — and hopefully our government will change its legislation to reflect a society that does allow for an equal division of labour and responsibility between parents. Until then — and once you are there and ready — I promise you that finding out what your thing is and physically practicing it will keep you from being sent over the edge by that mental note that only you carry about requiring one box of spaghetti to feed your family.

CHAPTER 4

Lisa Colalillo

FIND LISA: @LISAINTHECITY

Why be a lady when you can be a Queen!?

I'm writing this chapter because no one in my house listens to me.

It's not their fault though, it's mine, 'cause I'm only able to reach the octave they can hear when I completely lose my shit.

Also, I'm pissed. 'Cause before you have kids, women will say things to you like, "Your priorities are gonna change when you become a mom," or "Sleep as much as you can now," or "You're gonna need diapers later" — but not one single person told me about what would be my biggest struggle of all. It wasn't getting only a few hours of sleep at a time and turning into a zombie, or seeing my body blossom into a deflated balloon. It wasn't even discovering that I now had Medusa boobs that hardened and engorged to stone boulders — although all of the above so graciously contributed to my demise.

It was the identity crisis. Nobody let me in on the silent pledge of motherhood: that the millisecond you pop out your baby, the person who you've known yourself to be disappears. Poof! You enter into a world where everyone so generously slaps you around with their opinions and advice on how you should be doing life and parenting your babies: what you can now say and not say, how you should now do things and how you should not do things, what you should now wear and what you should not wear. Before I knew it, I was having a full-blown identity crisis.

I'm Lisa, an Entertainer / Content Creator / Host of GIRLtalk and a heterosexual, suburban mom who found herself again after becoming a Drag Queen.

I'm a big believer that you gotta change things up if you want to see change. I mean, if nothing changes, then nothing's gonna change, right?! And I really needed change. I'd been in a funk for such a long time and I started really noticing it after my second kid. It was at a time when I had finally gotten us all on a schedule and the survival mode of being a new mom had settled. It was like nothing specifically was wrong, but everything was wrong. I had started making sketch comedy videos on Instagram as an outlet to laugh at all the crazy things that moms go through, and it helped to keep me in a positive mindset, but the questions still remained. *Who am I now? Can I still have my dreams? What do I want to create for my life?*

I felt overwhelmed by the new role of "mommy" and frustrated that the possibilities for a woman with children seemed so limited by the opinions of others. I felt trapped and didn't know where to even start. Then, just like the magic you read about in fairytales, in came my Fairy Godmothers…well, actually, my Fairy Drag Mothers.

I had two Toronto drag queens as guests of my show, GIRLtalk. They were fabulous, glammed up, and sassy. They were *Queens*. And so, after the show, when they invited me to have a Drag Transformation, I didn't even think twice and jumped at the chance to feel some excitement.

We documented the whole thing on YouTube and Instagram, so when I say the makeup alone took two hours…honey, I've got the receipts! I'm naturally a brunette with thick, curly hair, but that day I was a blonde. I had silky, platinum Monroe locks and patent leather thigh-highs, my eyebrows lifted up into my forehead to create an animated and very theatrical character. I was a brand new woman. Poised and yet larger than life. I was a Queen! It was a complete transformation, but it wasn't just the makeup, wigs, and lashes. It changed me internally, and I found myself — and the new rules that I now live by.

The Power of Permission

Something happens when you do Drag. Aside from the new look, there's a new attitude (did you just sing that too?).

It happened the instant that I saw myself in the mirror with Drag makeup. There were sparkles and colours, and I was staring at someone I'd never seen before. It was me, but it wasn't me; It was my alter ego. Her body moved across the room differently, and her mannerisms were unfamiliar. Her chin lifted, neck long, shoulders pressed back. Everything around me started to look different. It was a completely new world! Looking back, the best way I can describe it is a state of being completely unleashed.

What fascinated me the most is how, in a snap, I could have such a high level of confidence. How was that possible?! I'm talking about a Kanye-level upgrade in confidence! Stepping into the clothes was like stepping into a vat of self-confidence and being chocolate dipped with sass. *Side note: I'm currently craving a Haagen-Dazs. Are you? Sorry.* It was an instant mindset shift. Drag gave me permission to act and think in a totally brand new way. What actually changed, aside from lots of glue and glitter? Nothing. An alter ego is like a portal to a totally new way of being.

There are so many examples of this, like how Beyonce has Sasha Fierce — that side of her that you see when she's on stage. Even my Fairy Drag Mothers, Xtina Monroe and Juicy, both shared in our YouTube series that their level of confidence comes alive when in Drag, and it allows them to explore a side of themselves that isn't available in every day life.

I once interviewed Todd Herman, a productivity coach for high performance athletes and entrepreneurs. He shared that early in his career he was insecure about looking too young, so he bought himself a pair of glasses with no prescription to look the part and feel more confident. Tapping into an alter ego brings out a new version of yourself.

Rupaul, the famous U.S. Drag performer and host/producer of Rupaul's Drag Race, has said, "We are all born naked. The rest is all drag." Think about it. How many times has getting your hair done or throwing on a red lip made you feel like a sexy and fierce mamacita?! Clothing and makeup is such a great tool for triggering a side of yourself to come alive. Creating your own alter ego can open the door to your confidence, your badass boss vibe, or even a demure, ultra feminine flirty side. Ooh lá lá!

RULE FOR LIFE: Drag made me realize the loss of identity from motherhood was in fact a blessing, and an opportunity to recreate myself into whatever version I choose — because it is a choice. Just as easily as I could place an order for a grande mocha latte with oat milk and sugar free syrup, I could place my order for who I wanted to be — and I wasn't feeling what I was currently choosing. The frustrated, suburban mom had to go. All I had to do was dress the part to generate that side of me.

Taking Up Space

The next morning I woke up with a sassy buzz from my Drag transformation, not to mention a basket full of used cotton balls from taking off all that makeup. But I could also feel myself slipping into my normal ways. How do I get that feeling back?

I remembered how I had felt in that moment of extreme confidence, and I was dying for it again. So I did what any girl would do: I had a glam session. A Drag glam session, actually. You should know that I have two makeup looks that I've mastered and just put them on rotation: a winged eye and bronzer in my crease…so to say my attempt at Drag makeup was a bust is an understatement. Was this the Walmart version of Drag Glam? Yes, but it got me there. And the second time, I took notes!

How do I bring this into my normal life?

It was amazing to get that rush from Drag, but how do I tap into that on the regular? The immediate change when I was in Drag was my posture, and it was the activator. Let me show you. Try this with me: Bring your shoulders down and back, elongate your neck, chin up, chest out and breath out a slow, calming exhale. This is the posture of a Queen. You'll feel more confident with your chin up and shoulders back than you will slouched over and very small. I've been binge watching an absurd amount of Netflix series about the royals, and if there's one thing you'll notice, it's that the Queen always has the same posture — no matter who's playing her. Her body language is poised and in a position of receiving.

Now that you're in place, with intention, think about your aura or energy. That invisible bubble around you that people feel in your presence. Expand it. Think about pushing it outwards and making it bigger. This is how you take up space, and how you take up space is the basis of feeling confident. The more space that you can take up the more confident you will feel, and the more far-reaching your vibe will be to those around you.

RULE FOR LIFE: Drag made me realize that I could activate the badassery inside myself by changing my posture.

Have you ever noticed how much energy you can hold? I never had, but when I did, I was more calm, more present, and held who I was with more pride and compassion. Confidence was the key, and it was just a little posture adjustment away. So chin up always, mama!

The Element of Play

Change can be scary, and motherhood is a big change. In all of the paths that my life has brought me through, motherhood has been the only one that so drastically changed me overnight (aside from COVID). It changed me physically, mentally, and all the other "-llys." When change comes, it can bring a heaviness that makes things feel so much more serious as you try to figure out this new life. For me that's where my bad funk began. Drag reminded me to bring the fun back into my life. Drag is about theatre and bringing your imagination to life. There's dancing and singing (well, lip syncing, but you get it). It's about full self-expression and fearlessness. Somewhere along the way I forgot to bring curiosity and exploration with me. I must've left it in my other purse, 'cause when I was in my funk, it was really easy to be scared of change. This uncertainty felt like one more thing that I had no control over, and when my mindset is serious, change is not something that I'm willingly jumping into.

But with a sense of play, change can be a curious adventure that pulls you to find a side of yourself that you never knew. It's an opportunity to learn and grow. And with *this* mindset, change becomes an exciting exploration into the new you. With play, it's much easier to jump into what life brings you.

RULE FOR LIFE: An attitude of play has become such a staple in my life. It makes life more fun and brings an ease to those harder times. When I feel myself getting anxious or too serious, the fastest way to shake it off is to literally shake it. Throw on the music and jump or dance in the kitchen, in the living room, with your kids, or completely on your own until you've shaken off all of that heavy energy and have a smile on your face. Bring play back and shake what your mama gave you.

These are the gems that Drag taught me. The experience enriched my life in so many ways, including the costumes they let me keep (yes, plural, 'cause I had to have a wardrobe change).

I keep the platinum Monroe wig on a shelf at my desk as a reminder to keep these elements alive in my life: the power of permission, taking up space, and the element of play. Will I do Drag again? If the opportunity presents itself, the survey says YES! But even if I never do, these new rules for life have been such a blessing at bringing a little more *life* into my life. I had spent so much time in the first couple years of motherhood exhausting myself trying to get it right by everyone else's standards. Then Drag made me realize: why be a lady when you can be a Queen?

Why be a lady when you can be a Queen?

CHAPTER 5

Elizabeth Cook

FIND ELIZABETH: **@LABRADORCOOK**

I t wasn't until I had kids that I ever thought during my binge watching of true crime dramas and serial killer documentaries, "I wonder how their mother must feel?" Now it is the first thing that I think about.

These days momming is just about as hard as it gets. We are stuck at home during a pandemic, homeschooling kids, working from home, becoming overstimulated, and desocialized with each passing day. If you recall, it was not always like this — nor will it continue to be forever — but right now it is a daily struggle. My kids hate virtual learning. I hate virtual learning. I am trying to work and I'm feeling guilty when I don't work enough. My house is a disaster because I just don't care, and none of us are getting the amount of exercise we need. I did not sign up for this hellscape.

Before the world went sideways, I had two boys in school — Senior Kindergarten and Grade 5 — and my husband and I both worked outside of the home. The weeknights consisted of karate, scouts, swimming, and skiing on the weekends. We call Bowmanville home these days and look forward to the time when we can leave home again.

I thought that I had grown up in your typical household..."typical" meaning just as screwed up as anyone else's...but that is not actually entirely true. An outsider might believe that they saw a family that attended church together every Sunday...they saw the children out playing with friends or playing sports. What they didn't see was behind closed doors and directly in front of closed minds.

I grew up in a family of five kids with my parents in a one bathroom house in Labrador. It is because of my upbringing that I decided I would have kids one day, even though I may not have enjoyed the presence of them — or rather, I didn't know how to act around them. I was the youngest (along with my twin) of the family, and I had never been in the company of younger kids until I was 16 and I became an aunt for the first time. Family can mean many different things to different people, but for me, children were a large part of that equation — a kind of necessary evil. My only hope was that history did not repeat itself.

Some people don't know that I have a brother. If they don't know that, they certainly don't know what happened.

My brother was the first born and the only boy of five children. He was a talented artist and athlete from a very young age. Chris started to have some problems when he was about 16, and from what I remember (I was 10 years younger) and have been told, he started using drugs and alcohol and having violent episodes. I guess my parents thought that his bizarre and out-of-character actions were a result of the drug and alcohol use, but when my brother was sent to Waterford hospital in St. John's, they were told that it was something far different.

Back in those days I doubt my parents ever would have admitted that they had a child at the Waterford Hospital. There were huge, negative connotations around Waterford that you would never utter the word. Mental Institution. Insane Asylum. These are the images that were brought to mind when you spoke about the Waterford Hospital. There he was diagnosed with schizophrenia. I cannot imagine what it must have been like for my parents, especially my mother, who still had another four children to worry about. His condition was never discussed. I just knew that he was sick somehow and not at home. Shortly after that he died by suicide. He was 18.

It wasn't until I had my children that I could empathize with how my mother may have felt losing her only son — her first born — and having no one to talk to about it. Mental illness was a taboo subject. You did not discuss it; you just hid it away. She retreated inward — a shadow version of herself, shrouded in shame, and lost in grief. When we lost our brother, we also lost our mother.

It was about this time, after Chris had died, that I learned the term "family secret," and I could not wrap my head around it. Was I just supposed to pretend that Chris never existed? That his life meant nothing? That he meant nothing? I couldn't do that, so I continued to tell people that I had a brother, and I was very open about the fact that he was no longer with us. My parents did what I guess they were brought up to do — act like none of it ever happened. I never heard my dad talk about my brother again. It must have been too painful, and he must have felt like a failure to his son and his family. He must have been scared to death that it was going to happen again to another one of his kids as we all grew older and challenged him, as kids do. Those same fears pop up when I consider my own firstborn.

Having children may have been an act of peer pressure within my group of friends. Once they started having babies, my husband and I realized that maybe it was time for us to as well. My first baby was a boy. I was terrified and elated. At one point I asked myself, "Did I just make the worst decision of my life?" It is hard to admit that I thought that, but it is the truth. As I sat there with my newborn, failing once again to sufficiently breastfeed him, I was worried that my past may have come back to haunt me.

Sullivan Christopher was an easy, happy baby and a crazy toddler, not unlike most others his age. Sully is now a funny and energetic 10-year-old kid. He will make you think about things you never considered before. He will make you challenge yourself and old beliefs, and he will drive you absolutely batshit crazy. I suppose I did know that being a parent would be a challenge, but I never realized that momming was going to be this hard.

As he was growing up, my family members would comment that Sully was just like my brother — how he looked and acted. I know to them that was a comforting fact, but to me it was the scariest thing they could say. I worried about him being like Chris, sick and uncontrollable, having to be sent away for the safety of himself and his family. Would I lose Sully the same way that my mom had lost her son? Would I be able to help him if he needed it? Then came the first time that my son said he was going to kill himself. He was five.

I admittedly freaked out and immediately took him to see a therapist. I felt that this was it, this was the sign that everything was going to turn out exactly as I had feared. On our first visit the therapist reassured me that this was actually an age-appropriate thing to say. When a child's vocabulary is still developing and they experience intense emotions that they cannot accurately communicate, then they will resort to saying the worst thing they can think of — "I'm going to kill myself." It was a huge relief to hear this, but it didn't stop the fact that we had a little guy with huge explosive emotions.

How were we to deal with that? And what exactly are we in for? I was thrown into a position that I was completely unqualified for.

Sully had been in a Montessori school since he was two years old. The structure there, along with amazing staff who had nothing but great things to say about him, created a solid foundation for him for when we would start school. He thrived there and had good friends. Then he started junior kindergarten at public school. If I had only known what kind of shit show that was going to be, I would have found some way to keep him in the Montessori/Private School.

School #1 — Within the first month of school I was called in to have a discussion with the teacher, Educational Assistant, Special Education Resource Teacher, and principal. They said they wanted to work with me and my son to set him up for success in school. We would have monthly meetings to discuss his progress. They continued by saying full-time JK was not mandatory, pushing that idea heavily on us. I made the decision to take him out for half-days only. Surprise! I never did receive another follow up meeting with the team. So, it was back to the Montessori school every day at noon to essentially nap all afternoon. I had seen an alarming difference in my sweet boy once he had started public school. Suddenly, he started with negative self-talk and his self-esteem plummeted. The self-talk was a result of what he had been hearing from the mouths of other students and teachers.

School #2 — French Immersion: The French Immersion school was closer to our house and within walking distance. I thought at the time that it would be a great fit for Sully. I admit fully that I was wrong. His teachers said he was depressed, had anger management issues, and I was being called daily at work because of a "situation." One day he was terribly upset before school even started and was screaming in the school yard that he was going to kill himself. I was pissed. I was at my wits' end; I was embarrassed for myself and for him, and I knew I would be late for work yet again because of this.

But when I was finally able to get him into school, tears streaming down his face, I saw two teachers whispering and looking at us, and I knew in that moment that I would fight for my child, regardless of myself and my ego.

I would fight for Sully so that he would never be whispered about again. I became very open about the challenges that we were having at school and at home. The evening tantrums that would come out of nowhere that ended with me having to bear hug Sully as he thrashed about, urging him to calm his breathing, all the while having visions of my own self, his age, being strangled by my brother while my mother tried her best to calm him. The constant acting out in school and how behind he was getting from everyone else his age. It was hard to admit these things. It was hard to admit that he was not perfect and that I certainly was not a perfect mother. It was hard to ask for help but through that open dialogue, we finally got the help that we needed.

I was upfront with the staff at school and I would ask, "Are we looking at ADHD here? You've seen it before; I have not." After asking this many times I finally got an answer in the most non-committal way: "It wouldn't hurt to take Sully to a pediatrician and see what they say."

I thought I would be relieved when I found out that Sully had ADHD and not the terrible, horrible thing that was created in my overly anxious mind, but I was not — because the reality was that it was now confirmed by a doctor that there was indeed something "wrong with him," and having that thought alone was an incredibly hefty guilt to carry. And the questions — oh my God the questions. Did I somehow do this to him? Did I do something wrong since he's been born? How will this affect the rest of his life? Will he take medication? Will he get addicted to drugs? Will he become a zombie? There was, and is, no end to the questions.

So, I did what I do: I researched the shit out of everything ADHD. I read everything. I tried every "natural remedy" from fish oil pills to essential oils to hypnotherapy, hoping to find the one thing that would magically help him get through the day. They were not magical. There is no "cure all" for ADHD, but there are many things that you might find helpful. We found a weighted blanket helps at night, a wiggle seat helps in class, and essential oils help to calm the limbic system when you associate the scent with calm energy and surroundings. Fidget toys are great, however every single one of them will be lost. I had stuck to my hard and true value that all medications are bad, so I did all of these things to avoid any type of drug. However, when none of those "remedies" could help him get through a day and I found that he was starting to fall way behind in school, I had to re-evaluate that "hard and true value" of mine. In that re-evaluation I found that it wasn't even my own value; it was a passed down family value that associated "drug" to medication. Even so, I still had a tough time coming to the decision to try a medication, but it was my family doctor who said, "If your child had bad eyesight you would get him glasses — the tools he needs to help him see better. This medication is simply a tool."

"Reframing" is a word you will hear constantly when trying to learn ways to harmoniously live with exceptional kids. I had to reframe a lot of things: my ideas surrounding mental illness and mental health, my feelings toward medication, and the idea that there is such a thing as "normal." The first day we tried the medication I watched Sully like a hawk, like I was expecting there would be some dramatic change in his behavior. He sat down and colored in a coloring book. That may not sound dramatic to you but that was the first time that he had ever picked an activity and stuck with it until he was completed instead of jumping from one thing to the next. I was amazed.

School #3 — Sully had gotten so far behind in French Immersion by this time that it would have been nearly impossible for him to catch up with his fellow students, and honestly, I got a vibe that they did not want to deal with this anymore. Truthfully, I was done with them as well. I felt like I was constantly fighting against the school for Sully. We transferred Sully to a school that hosted a gifted program and were fully equipped to handle exceptional students. Finally, we were in a school that accepted him for who he was, and because of that his confidence came back. When school was over in June that year, we were told they were not accepting any out-of-boundary students for the coming school year. I was devastated. Here, we had finally found a good fit for Sully, he was in a great environment, had met some awesome friends, and now I was being told we would have to go to yet another school? How could this happen?

School #4 — We unexpectedly bought a new house over that summer which was in a different school board district entirely. I no longer had to worry about him getting back into school #3 because now we were onto school #4. As it would turn out, this was the best turn of events that ever could have happened. It is a small school and the communication is great between the parents and teachers. I have not received one phone call about any "situation." For the first six months of school, I waited daily for the phone calls to come in. I did get one. It was to tell me what a great job Sully was doing in school and what a pleasure it was to have him in class.

Through the journey we had at school plus a new baby when Sully had just turned five, I eventually had to seek help for myself as well. This momming was just way too hard. I had first gone to see a therapist to get a better grasp of ADHD and to learn tools that I could use to help Sully. I also had terrible anxiety and depression and once I returned to work after maternity leave with my second child, and I was being harassed by my manager which amplified all the stresses that were already there. Again, I had to reframe those old, outdated beliefs that I seemed to hold so dear. I had to go on medication myself for depression. It was either that or I was going to quit my job to be 100% available for my kids and we could not financially afford that. I began to regularly attend therapy, which has saved my life. I openly talk about what I have learned in therapy with friends and family and I will continue to do so, so that they know this subject is never something to be ashamed of. I no longer fear the past. Instead, I look back to see how I can learn from it.

Sharing my worries, asking all of my questions no matter how "out there" they may seem, and creating an open dialogue about our problems and concerns are the most important things that I have learned in this journey. You are never alone; all you need to do is speak up. Sometimes that means screaming at the top of your lungs. Other times it could be a whimper. There will always be another mother there to listen, to help, and to offer advice if you need it. We are an army of mothers, battling wars every day, kicking ass and taking names, and there to tuck our littles into bed at the end of the day. To be a mother is to be a warrior.

CHAPTER 6

Elizabeth Desrocher-O'Quinn

FIND ELIZABETH: **@ELIZABETHANNESTAGING**

I struggled with how to begin this chapter — deciding where to start, what parts to leave out, and where to actually begin. There are so many factors that go through my mind when I begin to tell my story. It's not a simple story. It is a long story filled with a thousand heartaches, a ton of emotion, and it's extremely personal not just for myself, but for my entire family. It is layered with happiness and pain. I could write for hours explaining all of the ins and outs, but that isn't what I want to leave you with. I want to leave you with hope, inspiration, and a chance to believe that no situation is unchangeable. I want you to know that no matter how hard it is, I promise you that it will be different one day. If you had asked me five years ago if I could even imagine where my life would be today,

I would have never guessed or dreamed of where I am now.

My two blue-eyed babes are the number one things that I consider before I open my mouth and speak when people ask me what happened. Where did it all go wrong? Wow — that's a loaded question. Have three hours and two bottles of wine? When I read Courtney's call to action on Mummying hard, I thought about that. Is mummying hard?? Uhm hell yes!!!!! It's been so tough and extremely challenging. Well, actually, let me rephrase that; mummying wasn't hard. It was the situation we were in that was hard. My children were not bad sleepers or picky eaters. They did not have bad temperaments. It was nothing like that. I had a pretty hard pregnancy as I was sick every day, but then God graced me with amazing labours and little chunky, perfect girls. I say perfect because they were actually perfect. I was one of the blessed ones. They slept well and had these beautiful dispositions about them. They were kind, caring, and well-mannered, in a way that would make any mom proud.

Mummying became hard because I felt like a fake every day — a fraud of a mom and a wife. I was lying to everyone around me and pretending that I was living this picture-perfect dream life, when in actuality my whole world was crashing down around me.

When they were small and I was a new young mom, I also had my whole world shattered by addiction. There. I said it. *Addiction*…that awful word that took all of my hopes and dreams and shattered them into tiny pieces of nothing. A word that I was so naive about that it really didn't hit me until he was so far gone that he ran a stop sign, went through a red school bus sign, and landed on the front lawn of my children's school. Yep, you read that correctly! Proud mom moment right there. I was so naive that I thought he had had a heart attack. I mean, what else could have possibly happened to cause this?

It wasn't until I ran into the hospital screaming to see my husband and walked into his hospital room to find he was handcuffed to the bed! *"What the actual f***!"* is exactly what went through my mind. Then I quickly realized: *oh my God this is real. This is no joke. My husband is an addict and it has officially taken over my life.* The life that I had so longed to protect to make it look perfect. Our Christmas card looked like a postcard from a republican campaign. I was the president of the PTA. I was blonde, skinny, and had these two little mini mes following me around. I had dinner parties and never left the house without my 6-inch heels. How in the hell did this happen to me? My husband adored me. We had date nights and lived in the white picket fence neighbourhood with a ton of friends. This can't be my reality.

It was so bad that when I got to the hospital, the police didn't believe that I was the wife of the man lying there, foaming at the mouth, and not making sense. They were charging him with a drug-induced DUI. I was in shock and my whole world fell to my feet that day. They brought me coffee and asked what they could do. That wasn't even the worst part of that week. That same week, I was raped at a party, and decided to put our house up for sale. To say that life just stopped that day is an understatement.

I was in complete shock and had no idea what was happening around me. I don't think I even cried. By the time Saturday came around and one of my best friends came over, she knew that I was not well. I was in severe shock and she called in a favour to book me a therapy appointment the next day. I needed to be seen ASAP.

How was I fine going through the motions like none of it had happened? The next few months were a blur. I sold my wedding ring to get first and last month's rent for the girls and me. I had stayed home since Gracie was born, so I had no idea what I would do for money. I got a beautiful apartment in a very beautiful area so that no one would know that anything was wrong. Everyone would just think we moved. I sold my home and sent my husband to rehab not knowing if I would be getting a divorce at the end of this. The whole time

I told the girls that Daddy was just away at work. I ran his company to support us. His brother, parents, and my parents kept us afloat.

I was living in a cloud trying not to make any drastic changes, as the therapist said it would keep me from having a complete breakdown. I needed to be strong. I was all the girls had. Nothing mattered to me more than them. I spent my days trying to think about what the hell had happened. I remember my husband saying that I could come visit him in rehab. So, just like me, I got dressed to the nines, hopped on a plane, and headed out to be the supportive wife that he needed. It didn't matter that I was drowning in fear. I remember walking onto that concrete pad, 6-inch heels, a black skirt, and sharp-looking jacket: I wanted to make a good impression in order to show his doctors that we were good people and not scumbag addicts like you see in the movies or on the street. I thought it mattered.

Well, to my surprise, I walked into that concrete pad and saw the sign for "office." As I walked over to the door, the concrete pad turned into a huge jail-type yard where around picnic tables sat 90 men all looking at this terrified woman. I mean, wtf was I thinking? And then he turned his head and realized why everyone was talking. There was his young, blue-eyed, naive wife.

That was his first of three times at this one facility. Boy oh boy had my dreams been shattered again that day. I grew up wanting to be married young to a bald man, with two girls, living in a white picket fence neighbourhood, staying home raising my babies and having a husband that I adored. I literally had those words written down in my journal (I was a big Bruce Willis fan back in the day). That's what I thought when I met him. I thought I had hit the jackpot.

He loved me, he was older, he was successful, loved kids, and had a business. From there I felt that we were on the road to building our dream life. Little did I know that he had demons not even I could understand. We shared the love of so many things: our girls, our family, the church, and God. We genuinely had a strong friendship — and love. I thought that I would be married for the rest of my life. I would be the one who had it all and conquered the impossible.

Let me tell you something: nothing can prepare you for the shit storm that addiction can have on your life. If someone would have told me 10 years ago that my life would be destroyed by a tiny pill, I would have laughed in their face. The thing about addiction is that it doesn't care about your dreams, your ethnicity, your wealth, or your children; it doesn't care about any of that. None of it matters, because when that little pill takes hold...brace yourself for the worst ride of your life.

Ironic, isn't it...coming from the girl who never smoked a cigarette or ever did a drug in her life. I was the perfect victim to the lies, deceit, and pure devastation that addiction does to your life. Watching someone who is your best friend — someone you love — go through this is unbearable.

Then, watching your children suffer from the same betrayal and devastation is unthinkable. I am their momma. I am supposed to keep them from heartache and make their worlds as perfect as possible. I can't tell you how many nights I cried myself to sleep over what to do, and what the best decision would be.

When people say that they "stayed for their children" please respect that, as it's so true. How do you take away a parent they love and adore because you believe it's better for them? Try explaining that to a 5-year-old and an 8-year-old. It's not easy, and every decision you make to protect them feels like it is the wrong one.

There is so much in between the rollercoaster ride of living 14 years with an addict. It is a constant up and down that you want so badly to end, but you keep getting back on the ride expecting that *this time* it won't be as scary. That's the definition of insanity; doing the same thing over and over again, expecting a different result. That was my life, and it also sums up his addiction in one word: insanity. I gave this season, this marriage, this family all that I had. I did therapy, marriage counselling, rehabs, and left him twice, but it still wasn't enough for the strong hold it had on my husband. My babies are what kept me here. They kept me stuck, but they are also what pushed me to leave in the end.

Yes, the amazing thing about this story is that this isn't where it ends for me. This is the part where I find my strength! Where I get on my knees and pray for forgiveness and pray for comfort and strength and success. It's where I fight for what I know is my true potential.

My story didn't end with me never getting off of the rollercoaster. It didn't end with me crying in my sleep or ending up homeless (because that is where it was headed, had I stayed). I am so proud to say that it ends with me hitting the stop button and saying *fuck this, I want more. I deserve more and so do these beautiful children of mine.* So yes, I did end our marriage. It was the hardest decision of my life. I felt like a failure. I felt unworthy of God. I felt like I had been put on the secondhand rack, the one where you go when no one wants you. The used and full-of-baggage rack.

It took me a long time to realize that the word divorce next to my name doesn't define who I am or who I am meant to be. It does not make me less valuable, and it doesn't leave a stain on my children, because there is no way anyone should have had to endure what we went through.

I am proud of where I am today. I run a very successful business because my friends pushed me to do better and not settle for being stuck. I support my children. I own my home — and I am not done. I went from a desperate housewife to a successful business woman all from the depths of the pain and suffering from the addiction. No circumstance has to be a life sentence. Nothing has to be forever.

Life is a series of seasons. If I can get through that season out of the fucking window, then so can you. I am not saying it was easy, and that there weren't a huge amount of sacrifices and setbacks along the way, but it didn't mean that it was impossible or that I was ready to give up.

I want all of you moms out there who are struggling right now to know it's going to be okay — or it will be — if you choose YOU. In an emergency they tell you to put your mask on first, then help the ones around you. What good are we as moms if we don't take care of ourselves first? We must have a strong foundation and the strength to help our children.

Parenting while living in chaos is hard. Trying to hide them from all that is going on around them while still trying to keep your head above water is not an easy task. I wanted them to love their dad. Was I a perfect wife or mother back then? Absolutely not. I did the best that I could while trying to hide our personal life from the world. Did I do things that I wish I could take back or do differently? For sure. I was lonely and sad. I didn't realize that you could be in a marriage and still be lonely. That was something I learned at a hefty price along the way. However, like I said, we all do our best as parents and partners, and we all make mistakes. No one gives us a guide book on what a perfect home looks like — and quite frankly, I don't believe there is one.

I made a promise to myself the day that I held my children in my arms for the first time. I would make sure that they always feel loved and adored by me. I would make sure they know that I would lay my life on the line for them, and that no matter what life throws at us, we will always have each other. Today that promise has not changed. They know that they have a mother who loves them, and that together we will get through it all.

I truly believe that my bubbly, positive attitude that forgives so easily is what got me through this. There was no other option. I didn't want to take my kids out of their home, and I wanted to minimize any changes for them, as they had already been through so much. I fought to keep the house. I fought to grow my company in order to pay for it, and I fought to have a good man in my life who loves them — and me. I want my girls to always know that they have me in their corner and that I will do anything to protect them. I will always care for them and do everything in my power to give them the life that we all dreamed of, even if those dreams look different than they did at the beginning of this journey.

I am proud to say that, when writing this chapter, their dad has been one year clean, and we co-parent the best that we know how — for our children. We have ups and downs like many families do, but we are all healthy and on the road to recovery. My girls are thriving and adapting to life as it is. I know that they stand by me and my decision to change our lives for the better. They see the good that has come from the change, and they will grow up strong, fierce, and aware that life isn't a perfect fairy tale.

CHAPTER 7

Renae Fieck

FIND RENAE: **@RENAEFIECK**

The room was eerily silent. I sat there clutching my coffee, staring blankly at the book and journal sitting in front of me. I wanted to be alone. I knew that I needed to be alone, yet being alone was exactly what I was fearing the most.

The fear of being alone...forever.

Forever is a long time.

I had once thought that my "forever" meant a "happily ever after," and instead — in this moment — forever had morphed into one of my worst case scenarios. It's not supposed to happen this way, right? I'll admit that I didn't expect that life was going to be all rainbows and unicorns, but I didn't expect that *this* could happen to *us*. You never think "that thing" is going to happen to you. It might happen to anyone else, but it can't happen to us. Not our family. And then it did. Just like any event, whether it be divorce, job loss, mental health issues, or…the brain tumor, we just don't expect that it can become *our* reality — until it's staring you straight in the face.

It literally came out of nowhere. He was playing basketball one day, and the next we were faced with a brain tumor. We had been at a high point in life. I'd recently received the job that I'd been applying to for four years. We found out that we were pregnant with our third baby. And then this…

Breathe, Renae. Trust the doctor.

The worst possible situations flooded my head: *You'll become a widow with 3 children under the age of 5. You'll become the primary caretaker for a disabled spouse. You'll have to quit your job. You'll have to move because you won't be able to afford your home.*

And because I worked in rehab and I worked with patients just like this, I knew what the outcomes could look like, and so the thoughts spiralled out of control.

And then one beautiful thought arose: *this journey will become a part of your story.*

So I'm now here to share my story, because I thought that my husband being diagnosed with a brain tumor was going to be that "big" moment — you know, that one big obstacle in life that, once you get past it, you can share with others all the amazing lessons you learned. I thought that our story was going to be the typical obstacle, climax, and victory story like the books and movies portray.

Yet, for us, the tumor was just the beginning.

My name is Renae. I'm a neonatal occupational therapist, podcast host of the Rising Moms podcast, founder of the Rising Moms Club, and coach for women desiring to declutter their lives and focus on what matters most.

As I sit here and write, reflecting back on the day that I sat clutching my coffee, alone in the hospital waiting room, I can affirm that it was one of the scariest days of my life. The waiting as hour by hour crept by, followed by hearing the words "there was more bleeding than we'd anticipated," still rings in my ears. As if it were just yesterday, I can still feel the drop that I felt in my stomach the moment that I saw his facial droop — and I expected the worst.

I am beyond grateful to say that the facial droop was a result of surface level nerves, the bleeding was manageable, and the road to recovery appeared easier than we had initially anticipated. Yet, only three months after my husband had his tumor removed, I woke in the middle of the night to him seizing in bed. You always hear people talk about those primal moments when it seems like your body kicks in and takes action without your head really having time to think. I never understood it until that moment. It wasn't until a few hours later that the adrenaline waned and the fears came rolling back in. Once again I found myself waiting in another hospital room, clutching a book, as the reality of what was to come in the months moving forward began to sink in.

I'll spare you all the details, but needless to say the following year was one of the hardest years of my life, and by the time we reached our 10 year anniversary (exactly a year after Joe's brain surgery), I was done. I wanted to give up on motherhood. I wanted a life do-over. After 9ish months of being the solo driver for our family (yes, driving my husband back and forth to work, as well as kids to pre-school, and me to work), having three kiddos 5 and under, and working ~20 hours a week, I felt like I wasn't cut out for motherhood. *Was motherhood supposed to be this exhausting? How long was it going to stay this way?*

Postpartum depression! That's got to be what this is. That's why I feel so low and each and every single day feels like a hamster wheel of the same day on repeat, feeling depleted, running on empty, and quite honestly wondering if it was worth doing it all over again the next day. Being only six months postpartum, postpartum depression seemed like the feasible answer, right?

Yet when I looked around and talked with friends, the answer I got was: "This is just mom life. Mom life is hard."

gasp

Not sure about you, but that wasn't the answer I wanted to hear.

And as moms, are we ok with settling for this life? Are we ok with just accepting that mom life is hard and challenging? Do we want to just survive through the seasons? Becoming a mom has been one of the most incredible things that has ever happened to me. The sheer thought of raising, shaping, and giving life to another human being should be one of the greatest gifts we ever receive. Yet how can we do that to the fullest potential if we're feeling wasted, depleted, exhausted, and overwhelmed?

What if we are able to turn the tables, and instead of surviving, we are able to step into our purpose? Could we have the power to transform the world? Could we live lives full of JOY and raise our kids at the same time? What if, as a culture, we traded in the belief that mom life is hard and exhausting and instead saw motherhood as our refining adventure: the part of our story that challenges us to step into our greatest selves? What if what our kids need most is for us to be living into our best selves instead of sacrificing all of ourselves in the daily duties of motherhood?

I'll wholeheartedly admit that motherhood isn't butterflies and rainbows, but one of the greatest bits of wisdom I've ever been given that I will now impart onto you is "what you focus on grows" — the point being, you'll begin to see more of whatever your attention is being placed on. Tell me you've experienced the phenomenon in which you're wanting to buy something — say, a new car. You've got your eyes set on that gray Honda Odyssey and, just like magic, you begin to see them on the road everywhere. It seems like everyone has one. Now, there isn't all of a sudden a ton more on the road. It's the fact that your attention has now shifted to them and your brain has deemed them important. Your brain is brilliant in that way. It literally filters and processes information without you even knowing it. So when we're primed by culture and those around us to see motherhood as hard, exhausting, and busy, we're going to find all the ways in which to support that belief. But what if you chose to focus your attention on something else? Do you think it would be possible to start to see motherhood, as a whole, completely differently?

When I start working with a new client, they often describe themselves like most moms do: overwhelmed, busy, frazzled, exhausted, etc. Our culture has coined these phrases as the norm for motherhood. But what if they didn't have to be? What if we were able to leverage the fact that what we focus on grows — and begin to focus on something different? Most moms spend all day "doing," yet go to bed at the end of the day feeling as if they've accomplished nothing — spinning their wheels all day long, feeling like they have nothing to show for it.

But hear me on this: Motherhood doesn't have to be this way. There's hope for you to create a mom life in which you are thriving, living into the best possible you, and in which you wake up with joy each day. Motherhood has the potential to bring you life's greatest challenges, yet it also has the opportunity to bring you life's greatest joys. What I've found is that the women who focus their attention on those small joys start to see more joy in their lives, and we start flipping the script on this cultural status quo of "mom life is hard."

And it's not just me. Countless women have joined with me in going counter culture and creating a new way of doing mom life — and you can do it, too.

There are two things you can start with *today* to make massive shifts in your life:

First, you are already doing an amazing job. Do you realize that? When was the last time you stopped to scan your day for all the things you've done? When was the last time you took the time to find every single moment you've been *winning*? Maybe you got the kids ready for school on time, or maybe you yelled at the kids only once today. As moms, we often don't give ourselves credit for all of the little things. There's no one there patting us on the back, celebrating a job well done. We look at the list of to-dos and we feel like we've failed because it's not completely checked off. Yet, let's be honest — is it ever going to be completely checked off? And if we're waiting to celebrate our wins only until the list is entirely checked off or until we're doing life perfectly, we'll never feel good enough.

It doesn't matter that your challenging thing may look different than mine. It might not be a brain tumor. It might be a divorce, a child's illness, the terrible twos, or being a working mom. The challenge itself isn't that important. It's the way we respond to the challenge that makes all the difference.

When I reflect back on that year post my husband's tumor removal and remember all of the ER visits, the seizures, the ambulance rides, juggling life and work, and newborn life, on top of the countless sleepless nights — I'm surprised that I made it through. Moms have this amazing superpower to rise up to occasions they never once thought possible. Maybe it doesn't look pretty in the process, but you did it, and we do it every single day! Yet, we often do it without ever giving ourselves credit for the amazing feats we accomplish. We downplay. We compare the feats of our friends or the moms on social media to ours, and we see our own feats as not quite good enough. It doesn't matter the size or the "greatness" of the task. When we begin to shift our focus to the ways that we ARE showing up and ARE doing well, we can start to see all of the other ways in which life is pretty awesome. Mama, you need to celebrate and recognize all of those amazing things you're doing, even if they feel small and insignificant.

So take this pause for a moment. Repeat these words as a special gift from me to you:

> *I am amazing. Each part of my story and my journey has brought me to this place. The obstacles and challenges I've overcome have created me into the person I am today, and for that I am thankful. I embrace all of the obstacles that will continue to arise as my story unfolds. I welcome them, and I will be oh so thankful that I am able to rise above them.*

Repeat these statements as often as you need. Write it on your bathroom mirror, put a sticky note in your car, on your gallon of milk. Gosh, I don't care how many times you need to see it. This is how we re-write that story that says you aren't enough. The more you recognize where your life is amazing — where YOU are amazing — the more your life will evolve into the beautiful life that it is.

It's all about appreciating the small moments, which brings me to my next tip for you. You might have heard people talking about their gratitude practice. Especially in the month of November, with the American Thanksgiving, you'll see people nonchalantly listing out the things for which they're thankful. Yet, oftentimes, what I have found is that gratitude gets lots of talk without being fully embraced. When you embrace an attitude of gratitude in every area of your life, it changes things. It changes a lot, actually. If you and I were sitting down right now over a cup of coffee and you asked me, "What's the ONE thing I can do to make the biggest impact?" — it would be this. It's the secret sauce of life. Gratitude is what sets apart those who are truly happy and those who continue longing, never quite feeling satisfied.

Gratitude allows you to let go of things that don't serve you. It helps you embrace each moment, even the really sucky ones like brain tumors and seizures. Gratitude helps you find meaning and joy in even the smallest of things, and one of the most beautiful things is that it can change your perspective.

So much of our life is all about perspective. It's not about being Pollyanna and seeing life only through rose colored glasses. Life is going to have its challenging moments, trying obstacles, and hard circumstances. No matter how perfect you might be, chances are you're still going to forget snacks one of these days (or maybe even a lot of days). No matter how calm you might be, chances are you'll lose your temper from time to time.

Creating more joy in our lives isn't a matter of ignoring the hard or challenging aspects of life. It's not about being perfect or getting it "right" every single time. Creating a life you love that exudes joy is seeing each of those moments as *opportunities* instead of as mistakes, failures, or challenges. It's a matter of shifting your focus, letting go of that which you can't control, and focusing on those areas in which you can. I can't control when my husband will have his next seizure. I can't control whether my kids make great choices when I'm not around, or even when I am around. What I can control is the way I respond to each of those situations. I can control my feelings and thoughts.

I'm sure you can probably relate to being caught in the mental spiral. I arrived at preschool and had the fleeting thought of, "I wonder what day it was that I was supposed to bring a snack." As I checked the sign-up list, I realized it was that very day...yet there I was, unprepared with no snack in hand. I walked out of preschool feeling like a failure of a mom. How could I have forgotten something so simple as a snack? Maybe I wasn't balancing life very well. If I was failing at snack duty, I must be failing in other areas, too. And all of these thoughts spiraled me down so quickly into..."I'm a failure of a mother." It's amazing how something so simple as forgetting a few mandarin oranges and graham crackers can make me the world's worst mother. It's no wonder so many moms feel like they are a failure when such a simple mistake can send our thoughts into this downward plummet.

Yet — here's the beautiful thing! While you might not be able to control the circumstances around you, you can control that downward spiral. There's a lot of things in life that might be out of your control. Your thoughts, perspective, and showing up in gratitude isn't one of them. Those are within your realm. And those have the power to change the way you show up in your life. Those three things can allow you to go to bed each night feeling good enough. I know it seems simple, but without anything in my world changing, everything changed because my perspective changed. As moms we spend so much of our time trying to organize, manage, and control our external environments. We spend time managing the calendar, cleaning our homes, and supporting our kids.

Don't get me wrong. I firmly believe that the external stuff really does matter. For goodness sake, that's what I do. I help women declutter their homes, because your environment makes an incredible difference in the amount of chaos and stress that you feel, but I'd be lying to you if I said that a decluttered home is the biggest part of the transformation that I see women make. There's no amount of organization in our homes that can overcome the chaos of a cluttered and stressed out mind. So what would it look like if, instead, we spent the time changing our internal world first?

Mom life is this wild, up-and-down ride. It can throw us for some pretty crazy loops every once in a while — am I right? Yet, what I've found is that it's about the *journey*, and not reaching a final destination. You may not know what tomorrow will bring, or in what ways you might mess up big time. Gosh, if there's one thing that we've learned in 2020, it's that we can't predict even the most consistent parts of our lives. Part of enjoying the ride is releasing the control that we hold onto regarding what may or may not happen tomorrow — or even today. The other part of enjoying this journey through the highs and lows is learning to celebrate your wins, cultivate a life of gratitude, and control what we focus on. My friend, there is hope. No matter what season you're in, everything can change — and that change starts in the smallest of moments. You've got this!

CHAPTER 8

Andrea France

FIND ANDREA: **@MOMSNIAGARA**

It changes you. It changes every part of you. Everything you thought you knew. Motherhood. They say that when a child is born, so too is a mother, and there really couldn't be anything more true. Do you ever feel like you know what you're doing? Heck no. No matter how much research or prep-work you do, no matter how much advice you're given, nothing can truly prepare you for having kids. You are constantly learning, growing, and adapting. You're relearning and questioning everything you thought you knew — and it doesn't stop there. With every pregnancy and every child, your role and identity shifts and evolves. There is an ever-constant change of demands, expectations, roles, experiences — oh how the list goes on. And yet, there is a sameness in the daily — especially during a pandemic when you are particularly isolated — that can drive you a wee bit bonkers. Motherhood is a trip, and we are all headed in the same general direction. Side by side, mostly in our own lanes, tackling this wild ride one day at a time.

At 36, with two babies on my hips, one pulling my leg and one on the way, this is something I feel to my very core. Was this the life on my vision board five years ago? No, but I wouldn't have it any other way. Let me take you back a bit, when life threw me a bit of a curveball. When everything suddenly changed and I could choose to turn it into an opportunity for growth or start my descent down the rabbit hole.

It was December 2015, and I was preparing for the holidays with my then-fiancé of five years. We were all going to be travelling to Disneyland with his extended family early in the new year, right after I had completed my first step of licensing exams to become a Naturopathic Doctor. These specific exams were something that I struggled with; my Achilles' Heel, you would say. Even though I was a pretty exemplary student throughout my four years at CCNM and my clinic experiences at Brampton Civic Hospital and Sherbourne Clinic in Downtown Toronto, I had had to rewrite this specific set of exams more times than I would like to admit. With every attempt, my chance of success decreased, as did my resolve. With one month to go before my deadline, my then-partner decided to pick a fight with me, a pattern he had unfortunately exhibited prior to every single re-write attempt. This time, I was "uninvited" on the family vacay. Completely out of the blue, he said that he wanted to be married and have kids within the year, and with my primary focus on completing my professional designation, he didn't see that happening with me. I was shocked and heartbroken. I asked him to hold off on any major decisions regarding the trip and our relationship until after my exams. He reluctantly agreed, but it was clear his mind had already been made up.

In an effort to salvage my board exam attempt, I moved in with my sister and spent every waking hour, when I wasn't working or crying about my relationship, studying my butt off. To little surprise, although I was as well prepared as could be expected, I failed by a razor thin margin, once again. When I finally had a moment to process my emotions from everything that had happened, I didn't stop crying for 48 hours straight. It was my wrecking ball moment. My then-partner left on his dream family trip, while I babysat our two cats and began the process of moving out of my life as I knew it.

I took time to process it all. I hurt. I grieved. I took a good hard look at myself. While I hadn't been unhappy per se, I really hadn't been *happy* in a long time. I was compromising on so many levels, and I wasn't living my life for me. So I decided to make myself a priority for the first time in my life. I decided to do all of the following: to detox all that I no longer needed, and to start really focusing on me; to move my body in ways that felt good, through work and play; to fuel it with food that was good for me; to take big strides in my professional career and interests; to become a certified 200-hour level yoga teacher and further my scope at work; and to start enjoying my life. And you know what? It worked. I never felt better. I looked damn good. I was living a life of intention, for me. And I was attracting all the good things without trying.

After a few months, I decided I was ready to consider dating again. This really wasn't something I sought out, but something that kind of...found me. All of a sudden I remember getting a lot of male attention, and I was like *whoa, ok, hold the phone*. One night out, at the suggestion of a friendly drunken female stranger, I finally dove into the world of online dating. I had heard about it, but it wasn't really a thing when I had been single in the past. I wasn't looking for anything serious, so I was open to anything.

About two months in, on what was supposed to be the last date before I would commit to studying in solitary for the next round of board exams, I met my husband. Boom, instant connection. I had never felt quite the same way with anyone before. Tall, dark, handsome, he checked all the boxes, and the feeling was mutual. We were immediately inseparable. Fast-forward three months, and we were pregnant. Fast-forward three more months, and we were married. We had our son two weeks shy of the first anniversary of our first date. Without any intention or effort, and within one year of my previous split, I was the one married and with kids. Life is funny sometimes. I am so grateful for everything that has happened — all the struggles, all the failures, all the challenges — because they have led me to this pretty amazing life, one that finally feels like it's where I'm meant to be.

Despite all of my medical knowledge and training as an ND Doula, I was not really prepared for my son's birth at almost 42 weeks. I was pretty healthy and active my entire pregnancy (being a fitness instructor was helpful in this area). I had no real symptoms or issues, with the exception of getting kidney stones at 30 weeks — not fun and initially misdiagnosed as a UTI, but they passed. I had had Braxton-Hicks for months, but my early labour was completely non-textbook, every evening for hours for a week, contractions less than five minutes apart from the get go, etc. Everything was different than I expected. At the time, we were temporarily subletting an apartment in Port Credit while our build in Niagara Falls was being finalized. Due to the timing of our move, we were unable to secure a midwife, and even though I had planned to be as drug-free and natural as possible, if possible, when we had to have an emergency C-section it all went out the window. My epidural wore off during my overnight labour and our son's heart rate dropped. The next morning, I was frozen up to C7 with a spinal block mid-contractions, and I underwent major surgery. Despite the change in plans, I felt lucky to be under the care of my amazing OB-GYN, especially when things went south. Breastfeeding was something I was pretty dedicated to doing, and luckily we didn't have too much issue with my son.

Then came the first week postpartum. I feel like no one really prepares you for that first week, especially if you have to have surgery. Through all the courses, all the prenatal groups, all the chat groups, I remember thinking, *why did no one warn me about this?* Living off of absolutely zero sleep, driving to medical appointments while trying to avoid getting into accidents, doing everything to soothe your newborn while learning to communicate with them for the first time, trying to take care of yourself and your baby while being unable to sit up or twist on your own, having floods of emotions and bodily fluids, your swollen feet and legs slowly deflating from the size of watermelons while your boobs seem to make up the difference, having heated discussions with your partner while your baby wails at the top of their lungs...*just to name a few!* It is a rough ride, absolutely — and while I realize that everyone's pre and postnatal journeys are different, I felt like my emergency section really kicked my ass.

But we got through it. We figured it out as we were thrust into our roles as new parents. It was a strain on our relationship, but we made it through. My identity as I knew it had vanished. I went from being a strong, capable force, to a strong, capable *pregnant* force. But now I was just a new mother, with a major case of baby brain, spending every single hour of day and night caring for our baby in a new and unknown place, running on little to no sleep. I felt like I was losing my mind and my ability to communicate properly more with every passing day. While I honestly didn't mind one bit, I did feel a bit stir crazy, so I did what I could to get out with the babe in tow. Being born and raised in Victoria, British Columbia, I didn't have too many friends or family living nearby. Luckily it was summertime, so I would strap the baby into a carrier and go for walks along the lake shore, or I would meet with some friends from school. I made a point to take advantage of the local swimming pool, the library, mama fitness, and Kindermusik® programs before we moved back to Niagara. Being with other moms and their littles, even if we didn't directly connect, made me feel less alone.

That's when I had my first lightbulb. I had already been teaching yoga and fitness for GoodLife Fitness® for six years at that point. I thought, *why don't I combine that knowledge with some additional pre/postnatal specific training, and run my own health and wellness business in the Niagara Region?* I wanted to create space to help foster community, using yoga and barre classes as mainstays, while working with other healthcare providers to bring free/low cost workshops to local moms to really help create a collective. My plan was to eventually incorporate more of my natural health knowledge into the programming that I offered. I figured, why not put my varied skill set to good use? No one else seemed to be doing it at the time, and I was a new mom, so I had a good feel for what it was like, and I'd benefit, too.

Mama Bear Wellness was born. It took a couple months but then it really took off. I was running multiple pre and postnatal classes each week and continued to do so once I returned to my instructor job at the gym. Once again, my identity shifted. Now I was a *business owner.* I thought that if we had another little one, it would be relatively easy to run my side gig with a new babe.

I have one sibling, my lovely sister, eight years my senior. Even though there is a large age gap, we have always been pretty close, likely because we have a very small family, no cousins, no extended family — just my mother and us two. I knew that if I had kids, I ideally wanted them close in age. My husband is one of four, all close together, but he was willing to wait and spread them out a bit more. Well, life happened, and in January 2019 we found out we were pregnant with twins. (No, they don't run in my family, but they do now!)

Again, I found that I underwent another identity shift. Now that I was pregnant with twins, everyone seemed to treat me a bit differently than the first go. At work, random gym goers would feel more comfortable commenting on my body and trying to touch my belly regularly, without provocation. Of course there were my regular class participants who were always amazing, respectful, and supportive of my personal growth. They were like extended family. I'm talking about the complete randoms, who felt that they had the right to do what they liked. Being pregnant or a new mother is a weird position for a woman, where society feels that they have the complete right to comment, come into your space and touch you, or give unsolicited advice, especially in a gym/health environment. To be honest, it feels a bit backward. All of this weirdness has to have an effect on a mother's psyche, and even if it's only a random interaction from a stranger, it can stay with you. Luckily it didn't seem to affect me too much, but I think it's really something that goes unmentioned and needs to stop.

I believe that being active and healthy throughout my twin pregnancy helped a lot. While I did still end up developing gestational diabetes and super swollen ankles which looked like they belonged to another person, I was proud to be able to carry the babies to their full term of 38 weeks. I had rough morning sickness and vomiting that lasted every day all day for months. I did not plan on it, but ended up nursing my son all the way through until my OR date. The baby brain did seem to worsen, and while I suspect it was the result of nursing my son while growing two brains inside of me, I'll never really know. Even though our hospital was closed at the time, we were able to still have my OB-GYN for our scheduled section, which was a relief.

This was a totally different experience than my first. So relaxed, the surgeons joked around, and the nurses asked if we wanted pictures. If we had had some champagne, it would have been a party. Well, not really, but you get the idea. The twins were delivered and on my boobs in record time. All was good until they were tested and said to have low blood sugar. This is when an archaic protocol was put into place, where essentially we had to force feed them a gross amount of formula every two hours, all day and night. We would have to wake them up and attempt nursing for up to 5-10 minutes, but then we were required to give them a large amount of formula, much too large for their tiny developing stomachs. It was so much that they were clearly unwell, puking it all up. They were not to receive any additional milk until the 2-hour mark, when again, they were too full and/or sleepy to want to eat. I was told not to let them suckle for comfort, as it took too much energy and would contribute further to their low blood sugar. And so the cycle continued for 48 hours. Even some of the nurses agreed that this protocol was outdated.

This was the most frustrating experience that I endured with my children — to know what is best for your babies and to have it taken out of your control. I was losing my mind. My babies were about to completely lose interest in nursing. I begged and pleaded with my husband. While I acknowledged that doctors usually know best, I felt that this was not working for us. He agreed. We did what we needed to to stop the cycle from being extended. Thank goodness. Eventually I was able to re-establish breastfeeding. If not for my previous experience and knowledge with nursing, I would have felt completely defeated and given up. I am proud to say that I am still nursing the twins to this day.

Life with twins is busy. As newborns it was busy in a different way from now. There is constant nursing, diaper changes, and wanting to be held. Having the right tools was really a game changer for us. A couple examples are stacking two twin nursing pillows and having the appropriate twin carriers for when both babies want to be held at the same time, which still happens to this day. In the early days, I did my best to get out, but found it a bit harder with three children under three. Luckily I had a good friend, who would come visit, chat, and bring coffee. She'd bring her smallest little to play with my son and come hug a baby while indulging me with adult interaction. These are the friends who are worth their weight in gold. One day toward the end of my fourth trimester, we ended up commiserating on our love of coffee and wine, and our longing to just get back out into the real world and be people again.

Later that day, in the shower no less, I had my second lightbulb moment. Why not create a social community for moms that takes advantage of everything Niagara Wine Country has to offer? I could use some of the pre/postnatal connections and social media/marketing skills that I had already developed from running Mama Bear Wellness, while incorporating my familiarity with local wineries and coffee shops all over the region to start running community events for moms with littles. I wanted these to be events that every mom would love to attend. I knew that if I organized the events, I would have a better chance of being able to attend, with so many babies of my own.

I wanted to be sure that no one else was already doing this in Niagara. In my research, I stumbled across other groups in the GTA + Hamilton doing something similar, but no one was local, so I decided to reach out with my idea. One was away on holidays, but the other was encouraging, sharing her own experience and the benefits of being a part of the bigger network. At that point I wasn't sure if I wanted to do something completely on my own or as a part of a wider community. As I had baby twins and a toddler, I was unsure of the time I would be able to invest if life at home got busy, and I wanted to avoid being obligated for something that I considered to be a hobby at that point. I knew in my heart that this idea was pure gold. I knew I needed to take action. I would figure out the rest of it as I went, but leave the door open to working with the network in case things were successful. I did more research, registered the business, acquired the social media handles, and began bringing my vision to life. If Niagara Moms had been available on Instagram, that would have been our name, but here we are.

Moms Niagara, Inc. launched its first events, a coffeehouse meetup and winery lunch in January 2020, to great reception. Right from the get go, word of mouth spread like wildfire among local moms. I knew that I wanted to run a combination of free meetups, paid events/workshops, and giveaways that helped showcase local businesses, while doing something nice for moms directly in our community. I was able to juggle the business with being a mama by utilizing any time I could carve out. Building social media during any spare moments, while breastfeeding, moments while cooking, or late at night seemed to work pretty well.

In March 2020, our region was affected by the pandemic. Everything changed. We went into full lockdown. At that point, I had already run a number of different types of events, meetups, and giveaways and had more lined up on the schedule that had to be cancelled completely. I pivoted my Mama Bear Wellness classes into a virtual format, and found new ways to run events for the Moms Niagara Community, including our weekly Virtual Wine Club with The Wine Collectors Niagara.

The very same week, I had another company try to overtake my business and push me out. I had to lawyer up and incorporate my business at a less than ideal time. But I persevered. I took all of the challenges and the time during lockdown as an opportunity to reassess, to reconnect, and to refocus on my family — my why.

Now here we are, almost a full year since the pandemic started affecting us here in Niagara. It's hard to believe. Moms Niagara has continued to thrive despite the challenges, running safe and socially distant or virtual events when appropriate. I am so thankful for all of the incredible mamas, businesses, and brands that we have had the opportunity to get to know and collaborate with. I recently found out that we are pregnant with our fourth. The morning sickness has been hard and fast with this one, but I am truly excited for everything that's in store for 2021, and I can't wait for you to join us on the next adventure.

CHAPTER 9

Amanda Gurman

FIND AMANDA: **@HONEST.AS.A.MOTHER_**

Hey there. My name is Amanda Gurman. I live in Hamilton, Ontario, and I am a mother of two wild and crazy children who make me question my sanity on the regular. My son is four and his name is Connor. My daughter is two and her name is Scarlett. Outside of being a mom, I work full-time as a drug access facilitator at a cancer centre here in Hamilton. I am also a podcast host where I like to talk about all things motherhood. When I was young, I was not one of those girls who knew she wanted to be a mom. Motherhood was never something that I really thought much about until I met my husband, Chris. I became a mom at 27. I felt good about this decision at the time. *I felt ready.* I was married, bought a home, had a great career in pharmacy; I had done everything the "right way."

Having kids just seemed like our next step in life. Ha-ha, did you read that line up there? I felt ready. What was I thinking? I know now that nothing can prepare you for motherhood. You think you are ready, and you have an idea of what to expect, and then it's the exact opposite of everything you thought.

Motherhood is the most amazing thing that has ever happened to me, but it is also the hardest thing that has ever happened to me. Motherhood has tested me in ways that I didn't even know existed. Motherhood showed me my strengths, but it also revealed all my weaknesses for all to see — or it definitely felt that way at first.

During this chapter I am going to share with you the hardest parts of motherhood for me. The first is the transition into motherhood. The *"Who am I anymore?"* stuff and the *"What the hell did I do?"* thoughts. Yup, they are all here in this chapter. The second hardest thing for me was dealing with postpartum depression and postpartum rage after giving birth to my daughter. Battling a mental illness while trying to be a mom is the hardest thing ever.

After I gave birth to my son, Connor, motherhood slapped me in the face — hard. I had no idea that motherhood was going to be so physically, emotionally, and mentally exhausting. I was the first one in my group of friends to have a baby. When Connor was born, I remember thinking that life would be the same, except I would have a child with me. I quickly realized that this was not the case. We missed a good friend's wedding because Connor was ill one night. I missed every girl's night, every coffee date, everything that I was used to being a part of. That was hard.

The life that I once knew felt like another lifetime ago. I was up all night most nights, so going out just wasn't something I was up for doing. I can remember specifically sitting in my living room once just crying because I wanted to go and get a coffee and it just wasn't that easy anymore. In order for me to go and grab a coffee, I had to make sure Connor was changed, fed and happy so that I didn't have a screaming baby in the car the whole time. That was the moment I realized that my life was completely different. I was no longer the same person. This tiny human needs me all the time. I cannot just come and go as I please anymore. My life now revolves around this person and not me. Whoa. That was a hard pill to swallow. Once I got through the newborn stage, I felt like I had a little bit of understanding of this whole motherhood thing, until we hit a sleep regression. During this specific regression Connor wanted to be held in order to sleep. I can remember my mom saying to me so many times how she would always rock us to sleep every night; it was her favourite moment. I hated rocking him every night. My son was big, like 10 pounds at birth big. I was physically exhausted after rocking him for ten minutes, nevermind *all night*. But I did it. That is what good moms do, isn't it? My mom did it and she loved it. What was *wrong* with me? How could I hate rocking him every night? I finally got the guts to tell someone how much I hated it. One day my stepmother, Mary, was over and I told her. I was so ashamed. Her response to me was *"Okay, so don't rock him."* My mouth hit the floor. I couldn't do that. Could I? She assured me that I most definitely could. She showed me that being a good mom is when I am doing what is best for me. Happy mama equals happy baby. End of story. This was life changing advice for me. Once I saw that doing what was best for me was best for my son, Connor slept better, he ate better, and overall he was much happier — as was I.

The transition into motherhood is so hard. You can read all the books, prepare in every way possible, and you still won't be ready. Always remember that none of us truly *knows* what we are doing. We are all winging it day by day, just quietly hoping for more sleep.

During this chapter I also want to share my experience with perinatal mental illness — postpartum depression and postpartum rage, specifically. We are told at our 6-week check-up (IF you get one) that if we are feeling sad, crying all the time, or want to hurt ourselves or our children, we should get help. I did not fit into any of those boxes. So, when my 6-week check-up came, I told my doctor no, I was not experiencing any of those symptoms and off I went, thinking I was just fine. I was not.

The day that I had my daughter was one of the happiest days of my life. She was perfect in every way, and I was so excited to have her complete our family. The first few weeks went by and they were tough, but nothing that I had not experienced with my son. When Scarlett was nine weeks old, my husband went back to work and I quickly seemed to settle into the stay-at-home mom life. I was doing really great until the sleep deprivation caught up with me. I realized that I couldn't sleep when the baby was sleeping because I had a toddler running around who also needed me. My days were long. I hated when my husband left. I felt trapped being within our home. I hated my husband for working. I was envious that he got to leave, see adults, and not have to be a dad for eight hours.

I started to hate pretty much everything, even being a mom. My behaviour changed so much and so fast. I was snappy with my toddler and mean to my husband. When my daughter cried in the night for her feeding, it would enrage me. I still struggle to say that out loud. She was four months old and I hated when she cried. *What kind of mother are you?* I would think to myself. *Your children deserve better than you.* These thoughts would overwhelm me more than I could ever explain. I was stuck in this vicious cycle of getting angry, screaming, feeling horrible, saying I'll do better the next day, and I wouldn't. I just continued to hate myself more and more. When Scarlett would have a bad night, I would turn it into a bad next day. I started to dread every day that I woke up. Finally one day it hit me. I don't know who I am anymore. How did this happen to me? This is supposed to be the most exciting time of my life and I am not happy. WTF is wrong with me? I hated my day-to-day life, honestly. I would curl up in my son's bed with him reminiscing the days of it being just him, and how easy it was, and how happy I was back then.

I wished I could have gone back, but I couldn't. I had to fix this. My children deserved a mom who was happy. They deserved to see a mom who loved herself, so I could be a role model for them.

One day when my husband came home from work I told him everything. I said that I think something is wrong. I am not myself, I'm just…and he interrupted me and said "angry." His words cut me like a knife. I couldn't believe that I had become the "angry mom" — and that he could see it. I already felt like a horrible mom, but now I thought that I was also a horrible wife. He told me he had seen it for weeks but he didn't know how to help me. He suggested that I call my doctor, and I did. Within a few weeks I was seen by a mental health counsellor and it changed my perspective on everything. I learned in my first appointment that anger can represent both anxiety and depression. I had never heard of that before. This can be referred to as postpartum rage. My anger was coming from anxiety. I was feeling that so many of my needs were not met and I was not able to control what was going on around me. I lost myself and anger took over. I did not express that I needed help because I thought that when you're a mom, it's our job to put our needs behind everyone else's.

I struggled for a really long time with feelings of shame, and honestly I still work on it daily. I was so ashamed to be that "angry mom." I was so ashamed that I would lose my shit on my toddler on the regular. I was so ashamed that some days my baby crying would trigger me so badly. Moms shouldn't have to feel such horrible emotions. We are all doing the best that we can, yet somehow we put this expectation on ourselves that we will be the best mom ever. When we don't meet this expectation we blame ourselves, and the shame cycle continues. I had a name to my struggles and I was still ashamed. Postpartum rage. *Rage.* That word still gets me. It sounds so awful, but that was exactly what I was experiencing.

While I was in therapy my counsellor taught me many ways to cope.

She taught me how to calm myself down, how to express my frustrations with my children and my husband without yelling, but most importantly, she taught me how to be kind to myself during this time. I was doing the best that I could during this time, and that was okay. I learned about self-compassion and how badly I was lacking it. I think most moms do. You see, the transition into motherhood was hard, but this transition was harder. I think that I thought I would be better at it the second time around. I think because I already had a baby once and survived, I thought I would be okay the second time. I didn't account for the toddler who was awake all day, or the dishes, the laundry, and everything else. Once I wasn't able to keep up with everything, I thought I was failing. Turns out I am just like every other mom who's trying to keep her shit together on the daily. I just couldn't see that.

It took a long time. I stayed in therapy for just over a year and I am still a work in progress. Alongside therapy, I found so much peace in reading mom blogs that I found on the internet in the middle of the night while googling postpartum rage (which I did more often than I'd like to admit). I also met some pretty amazing women on Instagram. They helped me see clearly that what I was feeling was normal. They made me see that lots of other moms go through this too, and that I was not alone. With the tools that I learned in therapy and then some normalizing of my feelings with these other moms, I finally saw that it's okay to not be okay, even if you are a mom.

In my last session of therapy I had an "aha" moment with my counsellor. She had suggested that, since I was so impacted by these other moms, I should start my own mom blog. I thought this was a great idea. I got home, thought it over, and my husband suggested that instead of a blog, I do a podcast. In October 2020 I launched my podcast called "Honest As a Mother." My podcast is about normalizing all topics of motherhood. My podcast is a safe space for moms to come on, share their story with me, and then the world. I have had moms come and talk about breastfeeding struggles, what motherhood really looks like (it's really not all sunshine and rainbows, as evidenced in this book!), grieving the loss of a spouse while being a mom, and so much more. My goal with this podcast is simply this: I hope that one mom listens to my show and feels heard, and I hope that I can validate another mom's feelings like those mom blogs did for me.

So that just about sums it up. Motherhood is hard. Like, really fucking hard. If you want to question every move you make while making breakfast and picking up goldfish off the floor, then motherhood is for you. Just know that you always have a tribe behind you, because we are all tired, we all struggle, and we all can't stand our children from time to time — and that is okay. Becoming a mom is hard. Finding that balance of who you were and who you are now is also very hard. Battling a mental illness while trying to be a good mom? Really hard. But we get it done. After all, we are moms, right?

CHAPTER 10

Jennifer Hoffmeister

FIND JENNIFER: **@JEN_HOFFMEISTER_**

"That's unfair!"

"You're too bossy."

"I hate you."

"Daddy was more fun than you."

It's a good thing I don't keep track of how often I hear these phrases. Not that they are said all the time, but I have heard all of them more than once in the past year-and-a-half.

See here's the thing...I always have to be the bad guy.

I am always the one saying "No."

I never, ok *rarely*, am afforded the opportunity to be the good guy.

Every single time I have to make the hard decisions. I can't pass them off to someone else once in a while. I never have back up in making them. I can't say, "We both agree that this is what's happening," and with kids who so closely mirror my know-it-all, question everything personality, each and every "no" is met with resistance. Each one I have to justify to a five year old and an eight year old. I try the "because I said so" line that my parents would use to shut down the conversation — except it doesn't seem to work so well with my own children.

Maybe it's because they are so much like me. I mean, I was called "Mouth" by my father due to my need to always talk back. Maybe it's because they can tell I'm exhausted, and that even if I really mean no, they know that I'm just so spent from always having to say it that if they fight it, they have a chance to wear me down enough to give in.

Who knows? I barely have the mental capacity to try to figure it out.

My name is Jen. I'm an expat from the US living in Toronto. I came here for love and ended up building a life here that, in spite of the tragic end to my love story, I can't imagine leaving. I'm a writer (still getting used to saying that one), content creator, aspiring podcast host (it will be in print so I have to do it, right?), Director with Beautycounter, heels dancer, and so many other things — most of which I share on my blog over at jenhoffmeister.com.

I mentioned a tragic love story, and if you don't already follow me on social media or haven't read *Self Love Club Vol. 2* (which you really should read if you haven't yet), you likely aren't familiar with the ins and outs of it. Don't worry, I'll get to it.

I think we can all agree that this mom gig is freaking hard. Raising little people is hard; that's something I have never questioned from the second I became a mom. I've always been really honest about my struggles with parenting. This chapter could cover so many ages or stages of my motherhood journey, but if I'm honest, the season that I am in right now is easily the hardest. It's the kind of story that is less frequently told, or even experienced.

I was privileged (or naive) enough to think that being a mother could not get much harder than it was when I had two littles at home and a husband who worked impossibly long hours and even took a job out of town for three months back in the Summer of 2017.

Well, that idea was completely flipped on its head on July 18, 2019 when my husband, Warren, was killed in an accident at work. In a matter of seconds, I went from being a wife — part of a partnership, a parenting duo — to a widow and solo parent (told you I'd get to it).

Sounds rough, huh? The stuff of your worst nightmares? It was. It was and still is awful, but honestly the beginning was all such a blur. I was in a fog and the boys and I were fortunate enough to have all the support we could ever want, so that we were able to keep going at the bare minimum. Believe me, I'm not saying it was easy — not by any stretch — but we managed, only to then, less than eight months later, have COVID shut down our world. The night before we were supposed to leave and drive to visit my family in Boston for March Break, I cancelled. I was worried about the borders closing and not being able to get home, or who knows what else. It all happened so quickly with rules and restrictions constantly shifting that I felt safest with us being in our home.

So here I was, told to quarantine alone in my house with my then four and seven year olds, cut off from every single support that had been with us since the day Warren died. Now don't get me wrong, there was an element of the early pandemic and lockdown that suited our little trio. We slept in, hung out in pjs all day, the boys were often in various states of undress, no rushing, no schedules. We could just be. Be with each other, feel our feelings without any timelines, no one lovingly watching over us to see if we might crack. As helpful and important as the support in the first months were, this time was equally so. I didn't think it was possible, but we became even more in tune with each other's rhythms and cues. We could tell when someone needed space, or when to offer a hug or a simple "I love you." Thinking back, it's pretty mindblowing how attuned to these things my two little humans are at such young ages.

Then as restrictions began to ease, we began seeing some friends, likely breaking the mandated bubble rules. But, as well as we had been doing, I was especially lonely as an adult on my own with two kids and, frankly, I was over the Zoom drinks and all the virtual things. Thankfully, it was late spring and summer in Ontario, and it was a beautiful one. Lots of beach walks, splash pads, park visits, and bike rides with some adult backyard hangs for me. Again, it worked for us. We were surviving — and in many ways, thriving — as best we could. I then began to get comfortable enough to bring in our sitter when patios were open to go out with friends a few times. Definitely not the once weekly sitter that I had finally employed about a month before things shut down, but it was okay and better than nothing.

We even embarked on our first two solo family getaways. I rented a little cottage out in Prince Edward County to take advantage of the beautiful beaches at Sandbanks Provincial Park and then Thanksgiving out at The June Motel in Sauble Beach.

As I'm writing this, I'm realizing that I'm making it all sound rosy and lovely, and you are likely reading this thinking, *"But Jen, didn't you open this acknowledging that momming IS, in fact, hard?"*

Life was far from perfect, as I'm sure you can imagine. We had stretches, especially as time went on, where I just didn't want to hear their voices. Where they would fight all day long. Where I would completely melt down, unsure of how we'd make it through this. Because while the world was simply grieving their losses from the pandemic (and I mean those who have not lost a loved one to it), we were grieving that on top of still being in the very new stages of our own trauma and grief. And especially for the boys, as with most children, their grief evolves as they grow and are able to better understand exactly what they lost.

Let's be real. All grief and trauma is an ongoing process. You don't ever stop grieving a loss like ours, and it takes different forms. Here I was, alone, processing my own grief, when I couldn't ever be really alone. Putting the boys and I through Zoom therapy was fine, but is not the same as being in-person.

Then, throw into all of it having to make the decision about whether or not to send them back to school in-person. This decision was weighted with all kinds of responsibility for people who co-parent or actually live in the same house and are a partnership. I had not one other person who knew me and the boys as well as Warren did; who had all of our best interests so completely in their heart, in a way that no one else could no matter how much they love us. Make no mistake, we are loved, but not in the same way as that of an immediate family unit.

I put off the decision as long as I could, but ultimately chose to send them back to school. I know I'm not well-equipped to handle managing the virtual schooling of both boys. I knew they needed not only their amazing teachers, but they needed their friends and that social interaction outside of our cozy little trio...and my mental health desperately needed to know that they were cared for and that I could breathe for a few hours Monday-Friday. I could work or I could collapse if I needed to, as long as I could get them picked up at 3pm each day.

So they went to school, and things went fine. Any anxiety that I had was quickly abated with how well they were doing. They thrived. It was no longer "dummy baby school" for Wyatt. According to his teachers he was so much more attentive, responsible, and engaged in the actual act of learning than he had ever been. Logan had been looking forward to going back and aside from some academic struggles (likely due to my low capacity for the entirety of the prior school year and our decision to not participate in virtual learning in the spring for all of our own wellbeing), he couldn't be happier to be back at school.

While there was that constant COVID anxiety that we were all being forced to live with, especially as a parent or caregiver, things were good. I chose to book us a Thanksgiving getaway to Sauble Beach, as I mentioned above. It was somewhere that I had been wanting to visit, especially after a couple of extremely rough three-day weekends over the summer, where friends were out of town or with family. We were on our own with most things not open and little to no plans, when in a previous life we would have either been at my in-laws' cottage or down visiting my family. I knew I couldn't handle an actual real holiday on my own at home. I didn't want to wait for someone to include us in their holiday plans, and I didn't want to risk putting anyone in the position of feeling like they had to choose between us and their family because they knew I was lonely or struggling.

See, we passed a good portion of the first year post-loss — and a number of our firsts — in various stages of lockdown. Times we would have been enveloped in love and our people we passed on our own. So a weekend away seemed like the perfect solution. We could still eat a tasty, traditional Thanksgiving dinner, and I wouldn't have to make it on my own for the three of us.

Even before Warren died, I travelled on my own with the boys often, but I was always meeting another adult or family wherever we were going. The travelling part — packing, driving, whatever it is — I have that down. But I had only occasionally stayed in a hotel alone with the boys, nevermind a supremely trendy and Instagrammable spot like The June, where I was the only parent with kids as young as mine. As amazing as the walks down to the beach, hikes, mini golf, and all of it were, my constant paranoia that they were being disruptive was real. Plus, it was piled high onto the weight of a holiday, one that I in no way wanted to be spending as a solo parent with my kids.

And thus is the even more impossible (if that's even possible) balancing act of being a solo parent during a pandemic. Figuring out your children's needs and wanting to provide them with the magic on these holidays and experiences that you as a couple had planned for and wanted for your family, but knowing that you are feeling next to no magic even though they deserve it is hard. Wanting to honour your own boundaries around obligations, but knowing in doing so that you are compromising the experience of your kids is hard. Because, through all of it, there is no other person to step in when you're feeling down or weak or done. It's just you to manage all the things.

I'll be honest, I've never subscribed to the ideal of a Pinterest or Instagram mom. Sure, I threw some Pinterest-worthy parties for the boys' first birthdays, but my goal has never been — and will never be — perfection. So the lowering of whatever "standards" are out there never bothered me. But this time, as Christmas approaches, it's just a whole other thing.

It's like we are only just now living our first holiday season without Warren, because last year we were surrounded by friends. Some of Warren's co-workers took the boys to their big union Christmas party since I knew I just couldn't handle it. Other friends got us our Christmas tree. We had an epic trip to Walt Disney World over Christmas Eve and Christmas Day courtesy of my parents. It was so different from anything we had done before, and while we all had hard moments through all of it, it was different in a way that suited us then.

But this year — 2020 — is the year of the pandemic that crushed all kinds of human interaction, and we are currently deep in the second wave of it. This year is like the universe decided that we needed a second chance of having a real first Christmas without Warren, because this year we won't be travelling to my parents' house — a first in the boys' lives and a first in my 43 years. This year they won't see their cousins and family on Warren's side because we live in a lockdown zone and the boys attend school and it doesn't feel responsible to put my in-laws at risk like that.

These are decisions that I had to make alone; where I had to, *alone,* weigh the health and safety of our entire family. I had to weigh our mental health and what these decisions meant for it. I had to bear the weight of the decisions on my own. Yet again, I was faced with just how alone I am in this parenting gig — and all of this is happening at a time that has so much stress and anxiety, and all you want is to be nothing but fun and magic for your children.

I'm straight up not feeling any of the magic. I didn't last year, either, which is understandable. But I could breathe knowing that we'd be surrounded by family who wanted nothing more than to provide the boys with some magic where I couldn't. Plus, we were at the most magical place on Earth. We couldn't lose.

But it was 2020 and we all knew what that meant: anything you could or would count on is likely gone. So I sit here, knowing what kind of magic my boys deserve, knowing what I want for them, knowing what their dad wants for them, and feeling completely unable to provide it.

In contrast with my desire to search for some simplicity in our life, I have made Christmas explode in every room of our house, buying anything and everything that will infuse a little cheer. I have booked no less than five drive-through or car-based Christmas experiences in the hopes that doing them will bring some semblance of magic or joy.

And through all of it I still have to sit here as Logan cries about how Daddy was always here at Christmas. I listen to Wyatt wonder if he could ask "Ho, Ho, Ho" (what he calls Santa) to bring Daddy back for a day, like in the movie Onward. Then there's a night like tonight, where we were making cookie dough and Logan just lost it (partially because he feels my depression seeping into every Christmas thing we do), and all I could do is stand next to him with a hand on his shoulder as the mixer ran. Then Wyatt put his hand on my shoulder too. All I can think is what a tragically beautiful moment it was of us each comforting the other, but how heart wrenching it is that a five and eight year old feel that they need to do that.

This is all really heavy, huh? And it's likely that a lot if you are new to me and my story. I won't pretend that it doesn't suck hard and that I don't have days where I sit here comparing my life to others' — thinking about how much I'd prefer their struggles to mine.

But here's the thing: as I sit here and think back to that beautifully tragic moment and the group hug that Wyatt initiated after it, I feel like in this mess of life and parenting alone through grief, trauma, loss, and a pandemic, I might have gotten one thing right. This has all taught me how important it is to honour our feelings and those of our kids. They can handle more than we can ever know, and while no one wants their children to have to deal with the kind of pain mine have had to endure, I'm thankful that our experience has made talking about our feelings the norm. We have learned to sit in the proverbial mud with each other. We don't try to fix it when one of us is sad or mad or having any number of feelings that are so often deemed "bad." I have a five year old who knows to just put his hand on my shoulder because he thinks I just need to know that he's there.

I have an eight year old that can hear a crack in my voice or see a look on my face and know to ask if I am okay. To me that is amazing — and while these were things I had, in part, tried to teach them even before our loss, our loss has forced them to come front and center and actually be integral to our survival.

So, I think the general consensus here is that…momming is, in case it hasn't already been made abundantly clear, HARD. I'm still learning how to navigate it through grief, loss, trauma, world-pandemics and different parenting stages. It's an ongoing work in progress for me, and for all of us. It's made more difficult by the fact that many of us have a multitude of other roles and responsibilities outside of raising small humans. I'm many other things besides a mom and a widow. I'm a former advertising account person, film gypsy, baker, and mom group organizer. While I don't do any of those things anymore, they have absolutely shaped where I am right now. These days I spend the little free time that I have talking about all things clean beauty, connecting with my Instagram community, dancing in my high heels, and writing.

CHAPTER 11

Michelle Hughes

FIND MICHELLE: **@THE_MRS_HUGHES_**

Have you ever heard a voice telling you something? A voice that only you can hear? I have. The first time I ever truly heard the voice was in a waiting room for a fertility specialist. I heard it say, loud and clear, "You do not belong here." And just like that, I felt an overwhelming sense of assurance.

I was sitting in a dark and dated waiting room, two weeks after a surgery that was meant to help in our journey to parenthood. I remember feeling emotionally numb. I was struggling to understand how much or how badly I wanted to be pregnant. As I sat, I observed the others. I have always been a people observer. I interpret the body language, expressions, tones of voice, temperament, all of it. The

men were exhausted and tuned out, each of them reading maga-
zines. The women were stressed, their faces showing all the signs
of fear and anticipation and disappointment. Their emotion was pal-
pable. Not one of them was reading, just staring. Finally, it was my
turn. As is often the case with specialists, these were not warm and
fuzzy appointments; they were direct and to the point, with the information hurled at you.

I barely had a chance to sit down in the room before I was told that
the surgery discovered endometriosis, and one of my fallopian tubes
was full of scar tissue beyond repair. I think I was supposed to feel
anxious, upset, and a need to do whatever possible to achieve motherhood — but I was resolved, totally okay with being done with this
process. The voice had assured me that I could walk away now. At
that moment, I could not and would not go through another proce-
dure. The two I had already done were terrible. The pain from the
first I can still attest to being the worst pain of my life.

I was the girl who never dreamt of being a mom or a wife. We never
really talked about having kids, but one day we talked about it and
both realized we were open to giving it a try. We were patient during
the process of realizing that maybe we needed to enlist medical support. By no means was the journey easy; it was highly emotional. It
made some relationships divisive and included several years of not
feeling connected to friends, family, and society. I can now identify
that I also built up a lot of resentment at not being able to be just like
everyone else.

We took time away from thinking about having a family and made
peace with the possibility of never having biological children. The
idea of adoption kept coming up, and we decided it was something we would like to explore. Who knew that adoption would be
just as emotionally and physically exhausting and invasive to our
lives, relationships, and future?

Our adoption story was very much outside of the norm. If you are reading this and are an adoptive parent, you could probably say the same thing. If you are in the process you can likely relate, as all adoptions are unique and challenging. The adoption process usually starts with application, interview, training, then home study. Next, you start seeking a match and placement of a child, which leads to a transition time whereby you get to know the child, have visits, then overnight visits leading to permanency. The process takes about a year, minimum, and for some, much longer. We had applied to adopt and were patiently waiting for what we were told would be months before the call for training. Instead, not even a few months after the application, we received a call that our son needed a permanent home. We were sitting on our front step when the voice told me, "you knew this was going to happen" — but I didn't want to hear the voice. I ignored it; I was scared. A good friend was at our house. We were in our driveway when I told her, and she said to me that this is where he needed to be; that it's the best place for him. She was right, but I was still scared.

For us, the previously described process started right away, and we did all of it in six weeks. Yes, you read that right, six weeks. We were training, participating in the home study, and doing visits — all at once. If you consider a typical pregnancy, you have several months to prepare. From phone call to move in, it was six weeks. We hit the ground running and have pretty much been running since.

Perhaps some years down the road my son may give permission to share his story, or maybe he will share it himself. I am not sharing our entire adoption story, as that really is our son's story. This chapter is not about the adoption itself; it's about the impact and trajectory that it had on our lives. This journey has taught me about motherhood, and myself, and how I really have learned to tune in, listen to, and most of all — trust that voice.

Adoption brings trauma, and a child living with trauma is something we were not prepared for at all. We were starting from scratch with a two-and-a-half-year-old. I spent two years in play therapy with our son working on attachment. Imagine a little child trying to make sense of their world, working to form an attachment that most children make in the first moments, months, and the first year after birth. It is not "cute" play, not much "fun" play — it's building trust and ensuring safety. It is helping a tiny human process emotions and feelings that are too big for their little bodies. It was hard as hell.

I knew not one other person who had adopted. I had nobody to share this experience with. Many of the people I knew had or were having children at the same time. However, I felt completely different. Everything that other kids and families could do with ease we could not. We were told to make our son's world as small as possible to make him feel safe and assured to let his world be predictable. In keeping his world small, my world became just as small. I started to wonder how it was possible to feel this way. I was exhausted, frustrated, and angry all the time. I felt like nothing in my life had any ease to it. I only shared this with a few people. They wanted to be supportive, but could only share from their experience (all of which was from having their own biological child).

Adopting a child propels you into this strange societal martyrdom, especially if, like us, you adopt from the public system. There are lots of empathetic eyes and head tilts with "aww" added. There's even a few "you saved his life" type comments thrown in. The message I internalized from all of that was: if people think you are this "savior" then you probably shouldn't complain. Let's also add that I felt very much like we had chosen this. Although the adoption route — and our path — was entirely unexpected, it was the best for our son. So again, I really shouldn't complain. Funny how we see it as "complaining," when it's really just us asking for help and being honest with our feelings.

I was struggling to identify as anyone or anything. The chaos of our home was impacting all of us, and our marriage. I felt constantly that I was failing as a mother, because as an adoptive mother of a child with his needs, I *should* be much better at this. I *should* understand it so much more. I *should* perfect this every — single — day. The thing was...I was mad as hell that my life was in this state, and I constantly questioned how I ended up here. Our son, by no fault of his own, was a really hyper kid. He was not the sit-and-play-a-game kid. He wasn't the imaginative play kid. Once he started playing something, it didn't last long, or if it did, he would be so unhappy when he had to stop. He only liked specific shows, but he preferred the same episodes over and over. These reasons, among others, made the days so long and made it even harder for others to watch him for us. Essentially, I was it.

I knew early on that my son had been prenatally exposed to alcohol. I set out on a mission to have him assessed for FASD (fetal alcohol spectrum disorder). I told his pediatrician that this was my suspicion, to which she replied, "What would be the point of having him diagnosed?" I was floored, completely. I couldn't really process it in the moment. I left the appointment with more wind blown out of me. I felt that I wasn't seen or heard, and I was afraid that this was what the rest of our lives were going to be like. I never returned to that pediatrician again.

I really cannot recall how much longer it was before I asked my family doctor what I should do if I suspect FASD. His response was, "You can't unring the bell." I wasn't able to acknowledge it at the time, but these instances were my first exposure to the stigma around FASD and the lack of knowledge and support available. I became determined to find out how to get this diagnosis and how to support it, while feeling even more isolated and upset.

Prior to heading into my journey, all I knew about FASD was negative stuff that had been shown on TV programs when things had gone incredibly wrong. I was really scared for my son and our future. I hit the internet. There was not much readily available back then, but I found information about a diagnostic clinic in our area on a .pdf file in a newsletter from a local agency. I emailed the clinic coordinator immediately. I was told that my son was a bit young for a diagnosis. I assured the coordinator that I had confirmation of prenatal exposure and basically let her know that we need a diagnosis. So, we were added to the list — however, it was long, and only ten assessments were completed each year. I anticipated a long wait, but at least I felt that I was getting somewhere. I began to learn as much as I could about FASD.

In the meantime, I continued to struggle. My son had extra support in daycare and we were prepping for JK, only to realize that he was not ready for such a big change. The hardest part for me was working full time; we could not afford for me to be home. My husband was a truck driver and was gone most of the time. I was doing this solo. The nature of FASD is that changes and transitions are hard, especially in the younger years. So all week I kept our routine solid, which helped him and drained me. There was no room for spontaneity or change. Then my husband would be home on different days for various lengths of time, and it threw everything off. The house was turned on its ear with not one moment of ease or fun. I was trying to be the best employee and the best mom under tough circumstances. It was not going well.

When we got the call from the diagnosis clinic, I was thrilled. It was, again, a lot of work and a lengthy process. Feedback day came and I found myself afraid of hearing he did *not* have FASD, rather than he did. We sat through the information and finally heard that he met the criteria for FASD and was formally diagnosed. I was completely relieved, then completely sad. It is so hard to explain to those who have never been through the process. You know your child is different. You do not want it to be true, but it is. You want a name for it; you want answers; you want resolution; you want help. I have come to learn that being a parent of a child with a disability is a regular journey of joy and grief.

What may be most interesting is that the grief is what brought forward the voice again. I had been plugging away for years, working, wearing my special needs mom exhaustion and professional titles as badges of honor, hoping people believed it and convincing myself that I did. I kept telling myself that I was capable of all of it. I was a modern, competent mom who just so happened to have a kid with FASD.

The thing with FASD is that often things fall apart. I call it the wheels falling off the bus. Things can be going well for a significant amount of time, but then things go south. My son was in grade 3, and I was working at a job that I really did enjoy and want, but I knew deep down that I could no longer manage it all — and most importantly — did not *want* to manage it all. I was getting calls from the school daily, my job was in long-term care, a 24-7 operation (which meant inconsistent work times). I had become incredibly insecure about my work, which had never happened to me before. I was comparing myself to how everyone else seemed to be excellent at their job, managing their home and work lives like champions, and I was the weak link.

It was Fall 2016. At work I had the pleasure of being invited to a lunch with Commander Chris Hadfield, the astronaut. We were offered the opportunity to take pictures with him. Once my picture was taken, I looked at it and the voice came back, loudly, and said "You don't look like you here." I sent the picture to my bestie who said it wasn't that bad, but I knew it was. I was always tired; I was always frustrated; I cried a lot. I began to wonder what on earth was wrong with me.

I decided not long after, before Christmas, to make a doctor's appointment. I sat in his office, as I had done many times before, and bawled. I mean *bawled.* He sat and listened as he had done many times before through the sobs. I stopped to catch my breath and he told me that he did not think that I was depressed. He believed that I was not getting enough help and that I had too much on my plate. He expressed that I had always had high pressure jobs, that my son was a lot of work, and some other things he knew from my history. He told me that it was time for a break, and the sobs began again. How can I not work? How do I pay the bills? I cannot do a leave of absence because I will obsess about going back and how the job is being done better when I am not there. He handed me a note and told me that I was getting a break, his orders.

I was so relieved, but again, conflicted. I held onto that note for a month and I kept going to work. I was still entirely conflicted about being the best employee and mom, and if I am not the "best mom of a special needs kid" or the "best employee" — then who am I? Then it happened again. I was at work having a conversation with a resident family member. I began to dig my thumb nail into the palm of my hand, as I was just so completely tapped out of being able to solve problems for everyone. The voice said, "That is it; you are done." I handed in the note, giving a month's notice.

I was relieved but still very quiet. My parents, husband, and best friend knew. That was it. I was ashamed. I was scared but I really knew that it was going to be okay, just like I did that first time back in that waiting room.

I ended up taking six months off. I was finally able to just focus on my son's needs. The school calls were far more manageable with nothing else on my plate. Our routine was simpler. For the first time I was able to just focus on me when he was in school. When my husband would come home the upheaval was far less because the stress of my work and schedule was no longer a factor.

I made the very conscious decision to learn more about myself and about FASD. I became passionate about finding and creating spaces where parents, especially moms of kids with disabilities, can be open and honest about their feelings and experiences. I want to share my experience; I want to amplify the voices of those with lived experience. I started to immerse myself in learning and training. I became a founding co-facilitator of a local parent and caregiver support group. I sought out people like me who understood the journey.

Most importantly to me, I began to share openly and honestly about the reality of my experience. I decided to start posting on Instagram first, which evolved into in-person speaking opportunities. I was honestly surprised at how much what I had to say and share resonated with people.

I have come to learn that the voice that started all of this for me is my intuition. It has been a powerful, prominent compass that has always led me in the right direction, and I am grateful for it every day.

Thank you for reading. My name is Michelle Hughes. At the time of publishing, I will be the mom of a 13-year-old. I work in the field of FASD and am a passionate speaker and trainer. You can find me on Instagram @the_mrs_hughes_

CHAPTER 12

Heather Hutchings

FIND HEATHER: **@FYNN.AND.FEATHER**

It's 9:58pm. My husband is peacefully sleeping, and the baby is all tucked in for the night. After tidying the kitchen, brushing my teeth, and slapping on some overpriced, deep moisturizing night cream, I am finally ready for bed and some much-needed sleep. I try to drift off to sleep, listening to the waterfall music coming through the monitor. Readjust. Flip to my right side. Husband is still sleeping peacefully. I start to think about all of the things that I didn't accomplish today. Deep breath. Doesn't matter, "there is always tomorrow," I tell myself. I hear a movement on the monitor. Flip to my left side. Check the monitor. Gah! Who turned the brightness up on the screen? Oh, he's just readjusting and smacked his foot off the rails. Turn off the screen. Readjust. I flip the pillow, take a deep breath, and again try to get some sleep. A moment of quietness and my mind feels calm. It doesn't take long for another thought to pop back into the quietness and calm. Only this time, it's not a thought about what I didn't accomplish today. This time, it's about all of the things that I said I was going to do this year, or even last year. It's the list of things that I was going to change, or accomplish, and ways that I was going to make my life better. Make myself better. All of these thoughts race through my head like a movie reel, pinpointing every insecurity that I have about myself, about my abilities, about my failures, and about me as a mother. Highlighting the fact that I feel like I'm a failure, that I'm a disappointment, and I'm not good enough. Tricking me into doubting who I am — and me believing it. Thinking that I don't even know who the hell I am anymore. It's now 3:42 am. Husband is still peacefully sleeping, my baby needs to eat, and I haven't slept a wink.

Ever since I was a little girl, I wanted to be a mom. I wanted nothing more. My aunts would call me "mother hen" at all the family functions. You could always find me herding my cousins from activity to activity. Eager to jump in and help, I was often mimicking and embodying how my aunts cared for my cousins. I dreamt of becoming a mom and how many kids I would have — boy first, then a girl — you know, so she would always have someone to protect her. Every birthday wish, wishbone win, 11:11 on the clock, I would wish to become a mom. So, on the day that I became a mom, I had no idea the amount of uncertainty, guilt, shock, and disbelief that I would feel in myself. I had no idea how I would be giving up who I was before mom and be forced to embrace the strength of the person I was becoming.

Hi! I'm Heather. I'm a wife and a mother — and a woman independent of these two titles. I'm also a nurse, a firefighter, and a mental health warrior. I am incredibly proud to be called mama and to be my amazing and supportive husband's wife. However, I lost myself when I became both. I lost sight of who I was before I became a wife; before I was a mama.

When I first started to see the information and graphics for Momming Hard, I was stuck somewhere in between. I am passionate about helping others, connecting with women and supporting them in sharing their stories, too. So many thoughts and stories came flooding into my mind when I joined this project. I thought about all of the things that I didn't even know could happen when you become a mom. I wanted to bring to light all of the physical, mental, emotional, intellectual, and social changes that women go through to bring new life into this world. Yet, when I actually put pen to paper, I couldn't write a single word at first. Then I remembered all of the emotions, pain, loneliness, and confusion that I felt when I became a mom. I knew that I needed to share this part of my journey not only for myself, but for whoever is reading this, who might need the connection and support in their journey.

I became a mom on July 28, 2019. My pregnancy had been uneventful. My husband and I bought all the things, painted the nursery, and even attended prenatal classes (much to his dismay, as he is a third-generation dairy farmer and had probably seen more live births than most). I reminded him it was our first baby, and as much as the process is the same, I am not a cow. The prenatal classes talked about the "active" and "transition" phases of labour, and that if I told my husband that I hated him, I likely didn't mean it. The public health nurse was kind enough to show us all the tools available to help if the baby was "stuck," like the vacuum or the salad tongs large enough for a caveman to use. During class, I overheard a comment from the gentleman behind us saying to his wife "or we could just get out the baler twine and jacks instead." I snickered, rolled my eyes, feeling for this girl who had probably been compared to cattle her entire pregnancy, too. I knew my husband had heard it too because he looked at me, laughed, and smiled at me as if to say, "see honey, I'm not the only one."

More slides were shown on how to support the baby's head, the benefits of breastfeeding, the difference between the cross-cradle hold and the cradle hold. On the last day of the prenatal classes we talked about what to expect when bringing our baby home. The lack of sleep, the importance of rest, purchasing stocks in your favourite diaper company — wait, that wasn't in the class, but I have seriously considered it since becoming a mom. Oh, and you might be a little moody. You might feel lots of waves of emotions but don't worry, that goes away. So, when I was four months postpartum and that moodiness, that irritability, and the waves of emotions still hadn't gone away, I felt like a failure. It made me feel like a "less than" mom, because it wasn't *supposed* to be this way.

My nightstand was filled with half full water bottles, infant Tylenol, the baby monitor, and a stack of books — books about motherhood. *What to Expect in the First Year* — I would argue that whoever wrote that one wanted to ensure our species survival for the next 40 years. I had books about baby leaps, and the "wonder weeks." I had a book on the birthing partner. Oops, that one just never got put away. More books just seemed to be collecting and piling up on the stand. But one night, through the glow of the baby monitor, I saw the stack of books. I noticed a theme, especially with these two books: *You Are a Badass: How to Stop Doubting Your Greatness and Start Living an Awesome Life* and *The Universe has Your Back.* They were books about not giving a fuck — and about reclaiming your life. There were a few more on how the inability to manage emotions didn't start with me. They were all books about self-help and finding your own life's purpose; ways to bring yourself out of a slump, depression, and to help you align with who you are meant to be. As I stared at these books, I realized that not only did I not know who I was anymore, but I had no idea how to connect back to *me* — the person I was before I ever became the two titles, wife and mama, that I am most proud to be.

My postpartum depression didn't hit me like a ton of bricks. In fact, it had crept in so quietly, similarly to the way that I sneak out of my sleeping son's room. Its presence was so quiet — until it wasn't anymore. I was irritable, annoyed, and unlike myself, but I thought it was just from a lack of sleep. I went into my nurse practitioner's office three weeks before Christmas because I was so tired. I couldn't sleep even when my son did. My muscles hurt. My hips and knees ached. Not to mention that I had constant headaches that made me cranky and snippy with my husband. This was four months postpartum and, quite honestly, I was not impressed at all with motherhood at this point. I had convinced myself that I had Lyme's disease because a tick had bitten me six months prior and all my ailments fit the bill, except for the irritability. I chalked that one up to being exhausted from the all—nighters we were pulling trying to keep our tiny human alive. I sat in her office begging her to test me for Lyme's disease. This is what it had to be, right? We talked about this and that, how it could be from carrying, cradling, and nursing my sweet babe. But then, as any good practitioner does, she asked me how I was feeling otherwise. I said fine. Tired. The usual. As my eyes started to water and a few tears slipped out, she looked me straight in the eyes and asked, "How are you actually feeling?" We did the Edinburgh postnatal depression scale, just to have it on file. As she was asking the questions, more and more tears began to flow, and the diagnosis hit me like a ton of bricks. There was so much that I had brushed off, pushed down, and didn't talk about out of fear, judgement, shame, and guilt. All of these different signs and symptoms, which all became so clear to me after her questions. I was diagnosed with postpartum depression, rage, and anxiety.

I had buried all of these memories, but my mind had no qualms about replaying them over and over again after I was diagnosed. I remember the night that I finally knew, without a doubt, that right now I'm not okay. I needed more support. It had been *a day*. I'm sure if you are reading this then you can probably relate, and may even be able to picture your own "day." Husband was away at work. We were going through the six-month sleep regression, teething, and my son's first cold all at once. Nobody was sleeping. Nobody was eating. I had just been able to put my son down for a nap, after what seemed like an eternity, just to have the dog bark at the innocent couple walking by outside. Yep…baby is back awake again! Repeat this entire process of constant comforting, crying, feeding cycle until my husband came home. Finally, I could have a break. I could shower, maybe even sneak in a nap. Nope! Baby doesn't want to settle for him either. It was a *day!*

It was about 2:30am at this point and I was up for what seemed like the millionth time trying to comfort my son. I was frustrated that I couldn't help him, that I couldn't figure out what he needed, and that every comfort tactic that I knew of wasn't working. Sitting there alone in the nursery, sobbing along with him, I suddenly felt this feeling of intense anger start to roll over me. I couldn't stop it as this rage crept up from my toes into my chest, and tightened around me like an awkward, unwanted hug. I could feel myself shaking. It was a complete out of body experience to me, and I wanted to throw my baby. I had clarity for what seemed like a tenth of a second, and I gently laid him in his crib. I sank to my knees and wailed. Of course, my husband heard this cry for help from us both. He came rushing into the nursery, sat beside me on the floor, and he just held me and our baby. In the softest whisper that I could muster, I said "I don't think I'm okay." We sat in silence for a moment and he whispered back, "No, but you will be."

I went to a baby shower for a friend shortly after that night. I didn't know anyone else there except the expecting mama. Everyone was so welcoming and chatted with me as if they had known me for years. I remember talking with this one woman, who I had met a mere thirty minutes prior, about how traumatic my birthing experience was. I ended my story with a casual "Yah, but at least he is here safely, right?" She replied, "Yes, he is, but your experience and your feelings matter, too. You don't need to justify it." Her response and compassion gave me so much strength to walk forward in mother-hood, and I don't even remember her name.

There are many things that likely contributed to my postpartum depression. I reached back out to my nurse practitioner and was connected with a social worker. By going to talk therapy, I was able to identify and work through the trauma that I felt with becoming a mom. Considering that I had an uneventful pregnancy, I had the expectation that birth would be nothing different. We didn't have a birth plan — as long as the baby was safe during the delivery, we were going with the flow. Even though this was my first delivery, I think I can say with confidence that what I experienced was nothing short of atypical and traumatic. My son had arrived safely, however, not without complications for me. I had multiple emergency room visits with a newborn baby, begging to see the OB before six weeks because something didn't feel right down there.

After talking about all of these situations to my nurse practitioner, I felt validated and understood. With the help of my social worker I was able to begin to identify what triggered my rage. I felt loved and supported by my husband, family, and friends. It was important to me to be transparent about this part of my journey. I knew that I needed to be an advocate for my mental health just as much as I needed to be my own advocate for my physical health.

I wanted to share with you something that a co-worker shared with me shortly after becoming a mom. This co-worker knew nothing of my struggles, or least I hadn't shared with her. Maybe she could see it in my eyes, or on my face. Or maybe it was just a coincidence that, during my darkest hour, she shared this message with me. It was a simple, handwritten note with no explanation. *Carry on, Warrior.* I placed that note on my fridge, and it is still there today. When I returned to work, she asked me, "Did you read that book?" I was confused, because at this point, I had read *a lot* of books. I said, "What book?" She replied, "You know, the one I wrote on the piece of paper for you." That note carried me through my first year as a mother, and I still haven't read the book.

This season of my life has been dark. It has been challenging, confusing, and lonely. I had become unrecognizable to myself. I was angry, all in a time that was supposed to be the happiest and most exciting time of my life. Maybe you can relate. You yearned to be a mom — dreamed, planned, imagined and waited for someone to call you mama. You thought of everything that you wanted to teach them, show them, and help them learn. Then, when someone finally calls you mama, you are forever changed. Sometimes, though, we are so changed that we forget who we were before mama. We forget to take some time and care for ourselves, too. We forget that we have needs and a purpose other than being mama. We lose a piece of ourselves, our identity, and the life before mama. To be honest, I really struggled with this. I felt stuck in this unfamiliar territory. I was missing the person that I knew I was before my son, and I am unsure of who I am now — as mama.

In this season of darkness, I have learned that it is okay to miss who you were before mama. It is also okay to feel unsure of who you are now. It is okay to be in unfamiliar territory. This is the beautiful messiness of becoming a mom. Postpartum depression doesn't define you — as a mom, as a person, or even at all. In fact, it can empower you. Maybe this chapter gives you strength and encouragement, just like a note from a colleague or kind words from a stranger did for me. I reached out for help because it wasn't just about me anymore. It was about my son. My family. This deep desire to be more and to do more. So, continue to walk forward, embracing who you are now. Remember who you were before. Learn how to be mama and to also take time for yourself, and just know that the people who call you mama love you — wherever you are in your journey!

CHAPTER 13

Jessica Mancuso

FIND JESSICA: **@TRUELOVETUTU @SURVIVINGTHE5IVE**

Childhood me: "I don't have ADHD. I'm coping perfectly fine. I get good grades. I pay attention. I can handle it all."

Adult me: "Yep! I definitely have ADHD. I am not coping fine. I can't handle any of it."

Most females with ADHD go undiagnosed; not me. I was diagnosed at the age of 12, but it didn't make sense to me. Now that I'm an adult, however, it's all coming together. It's typical for us as mothers to experience one or two of the following characteristics on a regular basis, but if you experience all of them, it is most certainly not common, can be very overwhelming, and you may have ADHD. I'm not a doctor though. I'm just a mom with a bunch of kids and a couple of mental health issues, so you may want to talk to someone with a little more experience and perhaps a medical degree.

I tried really hard to have this chapter make sense to everyone, but the truth is, it won't. It's hard to write with ADHD, for obvious reasons. It's also hard to write with five kids running around yelling "Mommy, can I have a snaaaaaaack?", "Mommy, what are you doing?", "Mommy, he's bugging me!" while also maintaining a household, co-parenting, managing my business, and being a present and loving wife. I hope this chapter will resonate with some of you and make you feel like you're not alone. Motherhood is fucking hard, and I'm here to remind you that you are enough!

My name is Jessica, and I am a stay-at-home mom of 5 amazing kids (who are sometimes assholes). I studied Early Childhood Education and eventually did a 180 and got a diploma in Broadcast Journalism. I was diagnosed with ADHD at the age of twelve, but was never medicated for it. I also suffer from depression and anxiety that I am now taking medication for at 33 years old.

There are plenty of struggles that come with ADHD, and as I've grown my struggles have changed. My impulsiveness as an adult isn't the same as when I was a child or teenager. My memory has shifted, too; I used to be hyper-fixated on dates and numbers, but now I have to check my calendar for my wedding anniversary. I'm sure these fun traits will change again as I continue to grow, but currently these are the ADHD characteristics that make momming a whole lot harder on the daily.

Impulsiveness

Raise your hand if you ever purchased something you didn't need or bought something just because it had a good sale tag. This is me almost every day. My husband calls it *shiny object syndrome,* but ADHD calls it "financial impulsiveness." I spend a lot of money on shit I don't need. Apparently things like diapers and food are more important than ecotank sublimation printers. You see, I get really interested in trying something — like, compulsively interested — and I can't stop thinking about it until I try it, so I buy it. Then when I get it, if I don't succeed at it right away, I give up. So to help curb this, I always ask my husband. I know his money is our money and I'm not necessarily asking his *permission*, although sometimes it'd be easier if he wasn't so supportive. But even him simply saying, "Let's wait 'til the next paycheck" helps. By the time the next paycheck comes, I've usually forgotten about thing A and moved onto thing B. The amount of unused equipment we have sitting around this house because I couldn't resist a sale price or I just *had* to try this new heat press is ridiculous!

Problems Prioritizing

Every mom has a giant to-do list at the start of each day. It's prioritizing that list that is hard for me. I have trouble prioritizing my needs vs. wants. I need to clean the kitchen; I want to knit a scarf. I need to make dinner; I want to try out a craft I found online. I haven't quite figured out how to make the best of this one. I have, however, learned to forgive myself more. It's okay that the house is a mess. It's okay to order takeout or have cereal for dinner. One time I dropped everything I was doing because my daughter wanted a pink room, and nothing else mattered until it was done. Life is more fun if it's filled with wants instead of needs. I do recognize that it puts more responsibility and pressure on the rest of my family.

My husband won't function in a messy house, but he sees things differently than I do. For instance, when the kitchen is a mess, he sees ten small tasks. I look at the kitchen and see one mountain of a task, and I go find something more fun to do. I have learned that if I break things into smaller tasks and fit break times in between, then I can get things done.

Poor Time Management Skills

I don't have a middle name, but if I did, it would be procrastination. Ever since grade school I've left everything until the last minute, and although it didn't affect my grades, it didn't help with my anxiety and it continues to be an issue in my every day life. Procrastination is so much harder with kids around. Kids thrive on a schedule and routine. Like, getting them out the door and to school on time. Why don't I make lunch at night? Why do I always leave it until the morning of? Why do I wait to do groceries until we are on our last bag of milk or slice of bread? Why don't I put gas in the car before the light turns on? I have trouble seeing beyond the now. I am so focused on what is happening in the moment that I have a hard time thinking about what is to come. I have a calendar on the wall and in my phone with alerts, I keep a daily schedule on the fridge, but I still cannot seem to make the damn lunches the night before.

Problems Focusing on a Task

Focusing? No problem! Unless it's something I don't want to do… and there are so many mom things that NO ONE wants to do! If it's something I like, then I'm the polar opposite. But with kids, it's hard to get them to do what you want, especially because you're supposed to teach through play and let them lead or some shit. This is where my motherly instincts battle with my ADHD. If the kids ask me to paint or do play-doh or take them outside, I have a hard time finding enjoyment in any of that. Beyond not finding enjoyment, I can't even focus on it with them. I am always finding something else to do within that task, which makes me seem un-interested, uninvolved, or distant. Even reading bedtime stories...I feel so bad, but I hate reading them the same book over and over, and I can hardly get through it. I know repetition is good for their brain development and early reading skills and what not but... UrGh BORING. It gets harder as the kids get older, too. They get into this stuff that I can't even wrap my head around. Fortnite, Minecraft, Among Us, WTAF?! But they are so passionate about it and they can fully tell when I'm not actually listening to what they're saying. I know they feel like I don't care, but I do, I really do...I just can't focus on it because it's not what interests me.

I run my own small business. I started the business after baby #3 was born, making tutus. Shortly after that I expanded to make custom shirts, decals, etc. I started doing it for my kids and fami-ly, but eventually we started running out of wall space and money for my creations, so I turned it into a small income. I find it easy to focus on fun orders, but the ones that don't grab my interest? Zero focus...and then it also goes back to that whole problem of prioritizing things. My small business is more for my own sanity than the income. The best part of ADHD is the creativeness that comes with it. The business allows me to have an outlet for all the ideas floating around in my head.

Excessive Activity or Restlessness

This is where I most relate to my children. I can't sit still and not be doing or thinking of SOMETHING. Restlessness is a big one for me. I always want to relax, but don't know how. As a mom the kids keep me busy enough during the day, so when they nap or go to bed, how come I can't chill? Why do I have to give myself more stuff to do? It's not that I'm physically restless. I'm mentally restless. There is like a little hamster on a wheel in my brain constantly running. I recently took up crochet and knitting 'cuz it keeps my hands busy and keeps my brain occupied and on track.

Low Frustration Tolerance & Mood Swings

This one was a big eye opener for me. We all have our days of frustration, especially as mothers dealing with our children's mood swings. After baby #5 was born, I was always angry! I was very short tempered. When I wasn't crying, I was yelling, and when I wasn't yelling, I was crying. It was a disaster in my house. I couldn't satisfy my ADHD cravings like I used to and it came out in frustration towards the kids. I couldn't believe they wanted another cup of milk while I was busy working on orders. Did you know that most adults with ADHD also have mental health issues? Yep! I had finally lost what little control I had on my ADHD and anxiety. This shift caused me to start anxiety medication. Truthfully, it was the best decision I made. It's not like my ADHD disappeared magically, but it made it easier for me to cope with it. It helped me to slow down and evaluate what was making me so mad, and then allowed me to take steps towards healing. I still get mood swings, and the dumbest things can frustrate the hell out of me...but it's not as often anymore, and I can usually feel it slowly climbing up, so I have a better chance of curbing it.

Problems Following Through & Completing Tasks

Ok, so for me there are two ends of this. I definitely have trouble completing things if a) it doesn't interest me or b) I didn't succeed at it the first time. I have craft kits that I started years ago that I couldn't bring myself to finish, but also refuse to throw out. I have unread books laying around because another book sounded more interesting. I have journaling projects that I started and never finished. I started Early Childhood Education fresh out of high school because I thought it was what I wanted. After my first year it got too easy and boring so I stopped attending and eventually failed out. I have a history of throwing a curveball into my life every two years just to keep things fresh and exciting. In my 20s I never had a job, a relationship, or a house for more than two years. It wasn't until I had kids that the two-year rotations stopped. I guess kids change enough that I didn't need to change my surroundings as frequently.

Hyperfocus/Hyperfixation

How does one "mom" when she is more interested in finishing her game level than changing a diaper? I must admit, sometimes my ADHD and the need to hyperfixate or hyperfocus on something wins the battle over my parenting. If I start something that I enjoy, nothing else matters until that thing is done. This is how we end up having cereal or snacks or take out for dinner. If I start a book and get really into it, I am walking around the house with my face in the book walking into walls, giving the kids copious amounts of screen time and/or free reign of the house. When I find something I like, I cannot let it go. I cannot watch one or two episodes of something. Once I'm in it, I am in it! I will sacrifice sleep to finish a season, and then those characters will live with me forever and their lives will become my life.

Trouble Coping with Stress

Stress and momming go hand in hand. I don't think anyone would argue with this; I think the issue lies in how we cope with it. I am like a child when it comes to stress. If my husband tries to talk about something important and it starts to stress me out, I just cover my ears and la la la. I can't handle it; I don't want to hear about it. I cannot solve these issues. But it's not fair, because we're in a marriage and have to share responsibilities and blah blah blah. Instead, I will now verbalize how I'm feeling, "Hi, this is stressing me out, can we try coming back to it later?" The kids, on the other hand, are a different story. I can't just cover my ears and la la la. Or can I??? When I'm having a particularly stressful day, I put on my headphones and listen to music. I can see them, but I can't hear them, and then I don't get sensory overload and can try to rebalance myself.

Remembering

Five kids, five schedules, endless amounts of laundry, and work to complete. This would be hard for anyone who doesn't have ADHD. I have an extremely hard time remembering my past. I also have a hard time remembering your name or the conversation we just had, probably because my mind was elsewhere. This frustrates the kids because we often fight about whether or not mom said something. I also forget the simple daily tasks, like brushing my teeth, washing my face, and showering. Now, hear me out! I have limited time to complete these tasks as it is with all these kids around. Let's say I have two hours during nap time to shower, right? Put the kids to bed, come downstairs...I haven't eaten yet. Before I can eat I need to make lunch. Before I make lunch I have to clean the kitchen. Before I can clean the kitchen I have to put on some music. I turn on my phone to load up music and there are Facebook notifications, so I start scrolling, forgetting why I turned on my phone. Before you know it, it's been two hours, the kids are awake, and I haven't showered. Okay, well, I'll shower after the kids go to bed. You can imagine what happens there. Same thing that happened earlier. I set countless reminders in my phone to complete tasks and usually forget anyway. I'm sure you've heard of the term "mom brain" and have probably used it a time or two. Well, this is like "mom brain" on steroids.

Have I lost you yet? Are you still with me? Fantastic! So here's the sunshine in my storm: Not every day is a struggle. Sometimes my ADHD comes to shine in fun ways — like wanting to try something new with the kids, or spontaneously building a fort and leaving it there for days because it's no fun to clean it up. There are ways to manage and make momming less hard. Here are a few:

You are enough. I said it before and I'll say it again — <u>YOU ARE ENOUGH!</u>

It is okay to ask for help! If you're so overwhelmed with things that you're finding you can't focus enough to function, ask for help! I have a fantastic support system around me that I rely on heavily somedays, but not everyone does. So if you don't, hire help. If you can financially manage it, hire someone every so often to watch the kids or clean the house so you can let your ADHD flag fly free for a day.

Learn how to forgive yourself! It is okay that the kids watched too much TV today. I'm sure they didn't mind anyway. It is okay that you ordered dinner three times this week. Next week will surely be better (or maybe it won't). It is okay to quit a project that doesn't bring you joy. It is also okay to fully immerse yourself in something that does bring you joy.

It's okay to forget things. You're not a computer. You will get around to it eventually. Try to leave room for the important things in your brain that you'd really rather not forget. Or if you're like me and forget dates, post a wedding photo in your living room with the date, so you'll never forget again.

Feel all of your feelings. They are all valid. It's not easy juggling ADHD, anxiety, momming, and the plethora of emotions that can come with it all — but when I remind myself (and sometimes those around me) that my feelings are valid, it makes me feel better. No one can know how anyone is feeling in any given situation. How you react and how I react to the exact same thing are not going to be the same. So just remember that your feelings are valid and give yourself some time to process them.

Talk to your doctor. I never expected my doctor to be so comforting and understanding about how I was feeling. If your doctor isn't validating your concerns, find a new one. You don't have to battle this alone. Even if medication isn't the right path for you — because it isn't for everyone — your doctor will have other great tools and resources to help you.

And finally, always be honest. With everyone. Your partner, your friends, your family, and even your kids. It's a lot easier to get through this when you're not alone, and the best way to not be alone is to include people in your struggles. If you think they won't understand you, try it. You will be surprised — kids included.

CHAPTER 14

Sabrina Martelli

FIND SABRINA: **@SABRINAMARTELLI _ BEADIAMOND**

I had my life all planned out. You know, the one where you excel in school, obtain a higher education, secure your dream job, travel the world, meet THE LOVE of your life, have 3-4 kids, become a part of the parent council, bake, and all the while you're not even breaking a sweat and you're making it all happen! Sound familiar? I believe each one of us mommas has our own version of "life all planned out" before we turn 30 (at least I like to think we all did).

In high school, I had already mapped out my professional trajectory while my peers were still doing their career testing and trying to figure it all out. I have always had a type A personality, so it made sense to me that when I became a mom life would function the same way, right? I remember as a teenager imagining that I would be married by 25, and would have my children by the time I was 30. I envisioned living in that big house, having neighborhood gatherings, and my children being those kids that listen to everything and behave accordingly (haha).

Yet here I sit, at 43, and it certainly did not turn out exactly like what I just described (shocker). I did not meet the love of my life, Ricardo, until I was 26. We were married at 31 and we did not have our first child until I was 34. Our marriage had its struggles at times while we tried to figure out living together, losing our single life, becoming parents for the first time (and then second time), challenges with our second pregnancy followed by my postpartum depression, and all of the other responsibilities that come with managing a household. I had my own personal struggles with self-image, an unhealthy relationship with my body, and an undying desire to be "perfect." I was always striving for more — but at what expense? That type A personality was not doing me any favors. I was not prepared for how inadequate I felt as a mom, and how it impacted my very being. The harder I tried, the more I was unable to meet "everyone's" expectations (or so I thought).

Here's the thing — while it didn't all turn out the way I had planned, I'm here to tell you now that it's okay. It is okay because being a mom is the most wonderful, exhilarating, profound journey you will ever be on. It is also the most challenging, questioning-your-own-existence, scream-out-loud-with-tears-running-down-your-face journey you will ever be on. It's okay because momming is hard, but it is also intricately beautiful.

I'm Sabrina, a Master's prepared social worker, entrepreneur-at-heart, personal development junkie, Success and Manifestation Mindset coach, and now — an author. Here is what I have learned about Momming Hard when it comes to the balancing of roles and expectations, your spousal relationship, and your self-worth.

If you haven't already gathered, I'll lay it out clear as day for you here — I am ambitious as all hell. While having ambition is an admirable trait, when you combine it with perfectionism, it can become lethal. So, here I was, a mom for the first time with my daughter, Gabriella, and I had no clue if what I was doing was right or wrong...and that scared the beejeebas out of me!

On top of that, I felt as though Ricardo was relying on me, so not only did I have the weight of the responsibility of this new little precious being, but God forbid I messed this up. All I had was my parents as a model, and I knew that I did not want my relationship to be like theirs. My parents did the best they could (as we all do when we enter into parenting). I love my mom and dad. The way they parented worked for them, and I have some wonderful memories growing up.

I knew as an adult, however, that I did not want to be in a partnership with the stereotypical gender-type roles. I saw how hard my mom worked; how she held a 9-5 job, came home, took care of the kids, cleaned, cooked, did laundry, etc. My dad was the quiet one who worked hard and managed the finances. These are all admirable traits and I will forever be grateful, but the inequities were certainly not something that I wanted for myself.

This was the first struggle in figuring out our roles. Ricardo had this belief that the relationship between a child and a mother is paramount. I translated this to mean that I had to become the "be all and end all" in the household — and while my intention was there, I physically, emotionally, and spiritually could not do this all the time. Don't get me wrong, he helped in the house where he could; he cleaned, he would change diapers, do laundry, he would play with Gabriella and keep her entertained — but, while I was struggling with my belief system of ambition and perfection, he was also struggling with his belief system. His beliefs were ingrained from his own experiences, whereby his mom was a stay-at-home mom and managed the household. Being a stay-at-home mom works for some women and is to be commended, but this did not, and would not, ever work for me.

So therein lies the first lesson that I learned in motherhood: both partners struggle with their own beliefs. You need to learn to identify your beliefs, work through those that are serving you versus not serving you, and communicate the above. If you can learn how to support each other rather than going at it alone, you will both be much better off. What I also learned was that, sometimes, the roles that you each expect of each other are not based on "stereotypes" or "gender," but are simply based on the level of confidence each person has in certain areas of a household — and life.

And so, we settled into a routine of roles where I took the lead in parenting and we shared the many household tasks. Ricardo, however, struggled with my desire to continue in my roles as friend, daughter, sister, and entrepreneur. Our belief systems continued to clash and we both fought hard (figuratively speaking) to uphold what we thought was the "right" way to do things. Then we had our second child, Matteo, and our roles were challenged again.

It was a difficult season as I struggled with postpartum depression and this feeling that life was just passing me by. I felt lost, without a life purpose, and I was questioning everything. I was tired of arguing for time: time to spend with my family without my children, time to shop for fun, time to hang out with friends, time to read, time to take a bath in peace. And so, I thought the answer was to immerse myself in being the "best mom" I could possibly be. I aligned my very worth with this role — and what do you think happened? You guessed it! Any error in judgement, any remark going against what I thought was right, and any circumstance that challenged this concept sent me in the opposite direction of where I wanted to be. In focusing my attention on this ONE ROLE, I neglected all other roles in my life. I neglected my spousal relationship, I neglected my familial relationships, and, most importantly, I neglected my relationship with myself. As you can imagine, this then impacts your relationship with your partner.

So, let us talk about being a mom and the never ending battle of balance between you and your spouse. Before we had children, our relationship was spontaneous! We only had each other to focus on, so there were many conversations with wine, late night snuggles, and last-minute trips. The notion of making love several times a week was exciting (there, I said it!!!), and being woken up in the middle of the night for a late-night rendezvous would not start an argument followed by hurt feelings. We had all the "important conversations" surrounding what our expectations would be when we started a family, intentions of date nights, and not neglecting ourselves and our partnership...and then we had our children. There is a reason why people say "your relationship changes after you have kids," because it does! There is no denying this, and I believe that the desire to fight this is what leads couples down a difficult path. This idea that your relationship "won't fall into that trap" is what sets you up for falling into that trap! So, I am going to say this loud and clear: you simply cannot expect that the relationship you had as a couple before children will work in the same capacity after you have children. This is OKAY! I am sure if I investigated further there must be a universal law about this! But, while the message is that your relationship will change and it's often stated in a joking manner, no one really talks about how to accept these changes (so you don't feel guilty that they are happening) and how to equip yourself with strategies to continue to nourish your relationship in a different way. What I will say is this: learn the *Five Love Languages!* Everyone experiences love differently, and if you understand your needs in this context and your spouse's needs, you will be much better off.

For us, we knew that we loved each other, but when our children were added to our unit, it felt like we were often in completely different books (not just on different pages)! This ultimately resulted in a communication barrier. You know, the one where you both feel you're right, it becomes a competition, and neither wants to give in, which results in the silent treatment, sleepless nights, or worse — saying things that you don't really mean.

And to top it off, let's face it: momming is tiring! As mommas, we worry about our children and the family unit in a different way. I am coming at this from the perspective of having a partner. I can only imagine what it must be like for single moms — bless you! I often feel like the last thing I need is to worry about my spouse too! I already have to remember where the kids placed their gloves, and their special blankie, and...and...and...I don't need Ricardo asking me where his wallet is! However, at the end of the day, when the children are asleep, my husband is who I turn to for support, solace, or a simple hug.

Learning the *Five Love Languages* helped us to communicate better. I learned that I value and respond to quality time, acts of service, and words of affirmation. Ricardo is high (super high!) on physical touch and words of affirmation. Understanding what this means for both of us and finding a balance helped us move away from the competition and silent treatments. As I write this, I cannot tell you that we have it all figured out, because it still rears its head. What I can tell you is that we are better at communicating, understanding, and respecting each other's opinions. Figuring out roles and expectations in a relationship is hard enough. Add little beings into the mix, and it is a whole new ball game. Additionally, your roles may change over time. Be patient, be flexible, and be willing to really hear each other, admit when you are wrong, and love one another.

A discussion about how hard momming can be wouldn't be complete (in my opinion) without raising how it can (and will) affect your views about yourself as a woman, a partner, a sexual human being, and someone with dreams that may not include their children (did she just say that?...YES she did)!

In order to understand how my self-image was impacted as a mom, I'd like to share some background history. I was always someone who was hyper-aware of my self-worth and how I viewed myself as a person, both in relationships and in relation to the world around me. Growing up, I struggled with self-esteem regarding my body, and this impacted me immensely through childhood and adolescence. I believed that my worth as a human being was inherently woven into my physical image. I often remember hearing the words "you have such a pretty face — if you only...lost some weight...weren't so heavy...weren't so big..." and so on.

As a result, two things happened: 1) My desire to feel accepted sometimes led to poor decisions and 2) my relationship with food developed into an unhealthy pattern of emotional eating and dieting. Even in adulthood, I continued to struggle. I acted as though I was fine with my circumstances, but I knew deep down inside that I was not.

When we decided to start a family, I made the decision that I would get my body as "healthy as it can be" before I became pregnant. I did all the right things: portion sizes, exercising, limiting bad fats and sugars, etc. I continued this throughout my pregnancy with Gabriella. Everyone praised me for losing weight and looking great, which fed into my need for acceptance.

...and then motherhood happened. I no longer "had the time" and fell back into old habits using the crutch of "I'm a new mother." Our relationship was stressed with having our first child, my body didn't feel like my own, and I was losing a sense of who I was as I was overcome in my role of being a mother.

And can we talk about guilt? Man oh man, is that feeling a doozy! Guilt around spending too much time with Gabriella and not enough time with my spouse. Guilt around wanting to sleep in while my husband takes care of our child. Guilt around not preparing a home-cooked meal. Guilt, guilt, guilt — it does a number on your self-worth!

So here I was, trying to navigate motherhood, my job, my marriage, my external family, my friends — and then we became pregnant with Matteo. This is where writing this becomes hard. Our pregnancy was difficult and required close monitoring. I ended up taking a leave from work during that time, which only further sent me down the spiral of guilt and feeling incapable. Our marriage was taking a toll with the stress, and the whole time, I was trying to hold it together for everyone except the one person who mattered the most — ME.

Then the day came for my scheduled delivery. It was traumatic, almost requiring an emergency C-section. My baby boy was delivered. He was fine and perfect, but required to remain in hospital for a period of time for continued monitoring as a precaution. For weeks following his birth, I lived at the hospital, in another city, only seeing Ricardo and Gabriella on weekends. Saying it was hard is a huge understatement. I cannot even begin to describe the turmoil that I felt. Yet again, I held it together. I held it together when I was alone with my Matteo. I held it together when I sat by myself in my room with no windows. I held it together when I had to have conversations with the doctors and nurses. I HELD IT TOGETHER.

Then came the day when I got to go home with Matteo, and I couldn't hold it together any longer. Reflecting back, I know I had postpartum depression, though I was never formally diagnosed. I lost all interest and motivation in everything but my children. All of my energy and effort went toward taking care of them, but other areas of my life suffered.

I was the unhealthiest I have ever been physically, emotionally, and spiritually. Then I had "that moment" — the one where it all comes at you like a ton of bricks screaming that a change is needed. I remember it clear as day. It was our 10-year anniversary, and we celebrated by renewing our vows in Mexico on the beach. The day was clouded with my unhappiness — with the way I looked and felt. When we received the photos the next day, I looked at myself in those pictures and that ton of bricks hit me. I knew in that moment that I needed to make myself a priority so that I could be the best that I could be for my children and for my spouse.

Today, I am not where I want to end up, but I am moving toward that direction every single day. I am learning to love myself and all of the amazing qualities that I bring to everyone I touch. I am learning to love my body and that my beauty is not defined by my physical shape. I am learning that investing in myself is not selfish. I am learning that I am — and will always be — a good mother because I love my children with my very being. I am learning to be a wife, a mother, and a professional. I am learning that I love my husband, and that our relationship is exactly where I want to be — and what I need. I am learning to put myself first and accepting that this DOES NOT MEAN THAT I LOVE MY CHILDREN OR SPOUSE ANY LESS.

I would love to hear from you! It is my sincere hope that in reading my story, experiencing my struggles, and hearing my triumphs, that you feel a sense of normalcy in this wonderful life of momming. I hope that you do not feel alone, and that, despite the struggles, you recognize the potential for growth, joy, and the sheer amazement at being given the blessing of raising your little humans. You've got this my sisters!

CHAPTER 15

Alexandra Nicole

FIND ALEXANDRA: @ALEXANDRANICOLEXO

I have always wanted A LOT of kids.

I'm talking at *least* four.

I wanted a big family with a house full of kids, pets, and noise. I wanted it to be busy, loud, and full. I always liked the idea of someone being home at all times. This is basically the complete opposite of my own childhood. Now, I would never trade my childhood for anything, but I wanted exactly what I didn't have.

Growing up, I was an only child and it was amazing! I loved that I had the best of both worlds. I could have my friends over every weekend, for the whole weekend, yet I also did not have to deal with sibling fights or rivalry, and I had my own space during the week. I have a large extended family as well, so there was no shortage of events that we went to either. It felt like every weekend there was some sort of celebration or reason to get together. Even though I loved being an only child, I would still always question why my parents did not have any more kids after me and whether they would ever have any more (I think I finally stopped asking when I was about 13 years old). As much as I enjoyed my childhood and all of the luxuries that came with being an only child, I always envisioned having a big, loud, chaotic family of my own.

My name is Alexandra. I am a wife, an elementary school teacher, an entrepreneur, and a mom to two amazing boys. Motherhood has been nothing short of rewarding and incredible, but it hasn't always been rainbows and butterflies. Here are some of the challenges that I have faced in my motherhood journey so far…

Expectations vs. Reality

Well…I felt like I had zero expectations; about pregnancy, about motherhood, all of it. That all ended when I was told that I would need to have a C-section. Then, I felt a complete lack of control. I guess because I had such an easy pregnancy with my first, I expected my labour to be smooth sailing as well. To be honest, I never gave too much thought about labour or delivery. I didn't find out the sex of the baby. I was happy not knowing when the baby would come. I was excited to just take all of the cute maternity pictures and buy baby clothes (FYI — gender neutral baby clothes are nearly impossible to find!). Basically, I was just happy to enjoy every moment that came with growing a little human. So, inevitably, when I found out that I would need to have a C-section, I was devastated.

With the news of requiring a C-section, all of what I wanted to experience went out the window. When I was 21 weeks along, the doctor told me that I had placenta previa and there was a very low chance of the placenta actually moving — meaning that I would, more than likely, have to have a C-section. I cried. I cried the entire drive home. I cried to my mom when I got home (because she was at my house waiting for the crib delivery). I cried again to my husband when he got home from work. I was devastated that now I would know exactly when the baby was coming and, more than anything, I wouldn't experience or feel all the feelings that I was supposed to as a mother. I felt like I did something wrong.

Even though I *felt* like I had zero expectations of my pregnancy, I *knew* that I had high expectations of myself as a mother. I wanted to experience everything that came with it. Call me crazy, but I wanted to see how painful birth was and whether or not I would be able to handle it. I didn't want to know when the baby would come. I was looking forward to not having any idea of when my water might break (if it even did). I wanted to experience what my husband would do if I called him in the middle of the day to say, "meet me at the hospital, we're having this baby!"

I now realize that the expectations I put on myself were unrealistic. As pregnant women, we are to assume that we will inevitably give birth to a baby — that's just what happens. However just because I couldn't have my baby the way that I expected I should — or thought that I should — did not make me less of a mother. It also didn't make my pregnancy, delivery, birth, or postpartum any less valuable and real. The thing is, it actually made me stronger! I had to face my fears of having a planned C-section, something that I absolutely dreaded. It made me wiser, too. Now I knew firsthand that nothing goes as planned when you're pregnant. Most importantly, it made me more appreciative of what my body and my mind could do.

Things Will Change

Change. It is inevitable. It is something that most hate, me included. Yet, it is something that we know is going to happen when we become moms. Truthfully, I don't think I was at all prepared for how much (or what) would change.

Of course I expected my body to change. I knew that I wouldn't be able to keep my "teenage" figure forever. I didn't notice many physical changes during pregnancy for at least the first 4 to 5 months. Most people didn't even know I was pregnant until I told them. I also didn't really mind my body changing. Again, I was excited to be a mom and everything that came with it — big belly (and boobs!) and all. And then, after giving birth, I expected my body to bounce back with ease — I mean who wouldn't want that "teenage" figure back? Just another unrealistic expectation that I put on myself — *oof.*

Your body isn't the only thing that changes. Your relationships will shift — and so will your identity. Emotions will run wild, especially those first few days (and weeks) after bringing the baby home. Motherhood has really forced me to slow down. Sure, you're probably thinking, *How the heck do you slow down when you have children, especially a newborn?* But the thing is, as soon as I brought my son home, everything slowed down. Life as I knew it started to become more about my baby and not about me. Adjusting from my former lifestyle to motherhood was a huge shift. Instead of working late nights or coming home from the bar at 2:00 a.m., I was doing late night feedings and diaper changes. I no longer got to sleep in on the weekends, or take long, hot showers. Doing my hair and makeup was virtually nonexistent, and staying home by myself with a newborn was, well…lonely. The little things I used to take for granted now were things that I wished and prayed to be able to do. Who would have ever thought that I would pray to blow dry and style my hair, but I did! Inevitably, my priorities changed too. I would of course make sure that the baby was fed, often forgetting to feed myself. I would (and still do) put his needs over mine. The problem with this is that being "mom" became my sole purpose. Although I always longed for that title/identity and loved everything that came with it, I felt myself starting to become nostalgic for the woman I once was. I missed the woman who could go out for coffee or dinner with her friends or husband at a moment's notice, or the woman who took vacations to exotic places regularly.

My relationship with my husband suffered because of this, too. We were both exhausted trying to navigate this new life. Our son's needs were obviously top priority for the both of us, but that brought a lot of resentment on one another. I hated that he got to get out of the house and live life "normally" while I was stuck at home all day, every day, in the dead of winter. He hated that I got to "sit" at home all day, every day, and not have to "work." We also had really high expectations of each other because of this. Daily conversations sounded a lot like: "Why aren't the dishes done?", "Why hasn't the laundry been put away?" Or, "Why do you get to shower whenever you want?", "How come you get to go out with your friends tonight? I haven't seen my friends in months!" Needless to say, navigating parenthood was hard. It was something we definitely had to learn — and learn *together*. Now, after a second baby and six years as parents, I can confidently say that we are succeeding (And not just at parenting, but as a couple, too).

Truthfully, though, I think that the change that shook me the most were my friendships. I'd heard from friends who already had kids that "friends without kids don't often stick around," but I never expected that to happen to me. I had the best friends! Friends that were as excited as I was for this baby and literally went along for the entire pregnancy 'ride' with me: taking monthly pictures, throwing baby showers, supplying pregnancy cravings, all of it. Never could I imagine that MY friends would no longer be my friends once I actually had the baby. I never thought that our relationships would change in any way. Now, I know life gets busy, and I know firsthand that sometimes days turn into weeks, that turn into months, but I wasn't prepared to lose friendships all while losing myself, too.

I think the expectations that I had for my friends might have been too high. I'm not entirely sure, but I know that some blame is on me as well. I remember feeling so shameful about my postpartum body, especially at that 6-month mark. I started to notice that my body wasn't going back to how it used to be, nearly as fast as I wanted it to, and I wasn't comfortable with it. I started to not want to go out or see anyone. I vividly remember cancelling lunch plans with a friend because I had nothing to wear and everything I put on didn't fit right. I still carry a lot of this weight (no pun intended) for some of these friendships dwindling. Looking back now, I still can't explain or even pinpoint what happened exactly or what went wrong, but what I do know is:

Sometimes things don't last, and that is okay.

New friendships will be born when you least expect it (and thank God for them)!

Change isn't easy, but it is often exactly what you need.

Confidence is key, even if it is so hard to love the "new" you.

Buy new clothes that fit properly. This will help with your confidence.

Communication is a game changer for every relationship and situation.

Mom Guilt is REAL

You will feel guilty over everything — at least I did, and still do. Mom guilt is real — like, really real.

As a mom, not only did I feel guilty for wanting alone time or time alone with my husband, but I would feel guilty for everything, big and small. I would feel guilty being out for too long at the grocery store. I would feel guilty for sleeping in. I would feel guilty for wishing for more sleep. I would feel guilty for thinking that I wanted a girl when I was pregnant with my second. Then I would feel guilty for even thinking that. I would feel guilty for wanting my son to hurry up while nursing so that I could drink my hot coffee. I was at the point that I would start to feel guilty for feeling guilty.

My mom used to tell me that it was okay for me to drop the baby off at her house so that I could have a night out with my husband. I would spend hours, days, (weeks?) talking myself into it. I knew that we both (the baby and I) needed it and that he would be okay (I would be okay), but I still felt guilty. I was supposed to be caring for my baby, not going out for drinks. Nonetheless, I would hesitantly drop him off at my moms and then, almost immediately after driving away, feel guilty again. Hearing him cry when I left also never helped. For the most part, the guilty feelings wouldn't last, but only after texting my mom a few times during the evening to reassure myself that he was ok would I start to feel better.

Feeling guilty about asking for a night off didn't last, to be honest. Now, having two kids (and raising my second pretty much entirely through a pandemic!!), I don't mind blatantly asking our parents to watch the boys, and I have zero hard feelings about it either. I know that it is crucial for my own health — as well as for my relationship with my husband — to have some adult time. It is, in fact, also important for the boys to have those experiences, too. I want them to experience being spoiled by their grandparents; staying up late, eating too much junk food, not brushing their teeth at night (grr), and mainly just building those relationships that I have with my grandparents.

One thing I have learned, though, is that mom guilt is one of those

feelings that will never really go away. Although I have more confidence in dropping my kids off at their grandparents so I can have some me time, I still often feel guilty for random other things.

Too much screen time today? Guilty!

Not remembering to brush his teeth before bed one night of the week? Guilty!

Not saying 'I love you' one last time at school drop off? Guilty!

Hotdogs and fruit pouches for lunch? Guilty!

Thinking that my son feels sad (even though he has no reason to feel sad, but I think that he might feel sad)? Guilty!

Guilt is such a funny thing because it's that pervasive feeling of not doing enough as a parent, or not doing the right things, or not making the right decisions. It's always wondering, Is this the thing that is going to "mess" them up later in life? Yet, literally everything I do (or don't do) causes mom guilt, and I have no doubt that this feeling will never end. I hope that my kids realize that everything I do, I do for them, and I hope that they will eventually appreciate how much I love every freakin' thing about them and want the very best for them — so much so that I even feel their feelings for them.

What I've Learned

I don't know if it's that my husband and I are just more "lax" or if we are now just more experienced as parents, but the adjustment of going from 1 to 2 kids was wayyyy easier than going from 0 to 1 for us. Again, going back to these ridiculous expectations that we, along with everyone else, puts on us as new parents, I feel like we just totally aced it as a team the second time around. All of those ridiculous things that people suggest or tell you to do with

your first is literally out the window with your second. I can confidently say that we did anything and everything with our second that would make OUR lives easier. If that meant that I stopped breastfeeding after four months because it was just becoming too hard or not enjoyable for my mental health, then I stopped — without hesitation, worry, or fear of judgement. If we found it easier this time around to feed the baby what we were eating instead of pureeing our own food because it was more convenient and what our baby wanted, then we did it. This inevitably builds not only a stronger relationship for us as a couple, but also as parents.

Our children watch every little thing we do, so once we stopped worrying about doing the damn dishes, or having the tidiest bedrooms — and started to focus more on building cool forts, having epic dance parties, and just making memories — things started to change. Our priorities changed. We, as a team, decided that whatever worked for US and OUR family was what we were going to do, and I think this shift of becoming a team was what made the adjustment from 1 to 2 kids so seamless. This is not to say that with our first we were never on the same page, or that we didn't make decisions that were best for our family together, but I do think that with the ease of already knowing what worked and what didn't with the first made every decision with the second easier.

So, what I've learned in my journey through motherhood so far is that expectations, rules, opinions, comparison, and guilt are all shit. We put so much pressure on ourselves as mothers to be the best, to do it all, and to know everything, all while taking care of and raising tiny humans. This is an impossible task for anyone; yet, if anyone could do any of it, it would be us moms, and that's why we do it. What I've come to realize, however, is that we can't be perfect — and we can't expect to be, either. When we start to overwhelm ourselves with expectations, opinions, comparison, and guilt, we then start to feel exhaustion, jealousy, animosity,

and that we aren't good enough. Instead, we need to just embrace the chaos, love the messiness, and enjoy these little people while they're still little, and while they still (somewhat) listen to us.

Momming is HARD. But I'm here to reassure you that even though it's hard as hell, being a mom is the most wonderful and fulfilling thing I have ever done — and I wouldn't change a damn thing.

** Oh, and if you're wondering if I will ever get that big family with four kids that I've always desired, my husband and I have decided on having two kids…for now.

CHAPTER 16

Nicky Nock

FIND NICKY: **@NICKY_NOCK_**

An Introduction

I grew up in England and moved to Canada 8 years ago now. Having kids was not on my radar for the longest time, as I was so driven to move to Canada and I was way too obsessed with my career.

It's funny...I always wondered when I would have a child. When I was 13 and started my period, I thought I would have a baby when I was 18. When I was 18, it was 23. When I was 23, it pretty much was nope, not interested!

In the UK, there is this assumption and stigma that pretty much the day after you are married you should be having a baby. Why do people ask that friggin question? "So, when are you guys going to have a baby?" None of your bloody business is the answer. After a while, they stopped asking. Hurrah!

I am a fitness professional and have worked in the industry for nearly 20 years. Honing my skill, being the best presenter, the fittest athlete, and receiving the most accolades was important to me from my early 20s to 30s. I got married one month before my 30th birthday, and I still was not ready to become a Mum. There was one more thing that I wanted to accomplish, and that was to become a Canadian resident.

I finally became a Canadian resident in 2013, three years after my husband and I started the process. I was 33. Was I ready to be a Mum then? Nope! But people started asking again, now that we had found our forever home.

I became a Mum in 2017. I was 37. Was I ready to be a Mum then? Nope!!!!! I don't think that you are ever ready! Do you?

Who The Heck Am I?

"Losing yourself is easy. Discovering who you truly are is a brave, vulnerable journey" -Nicky Nock

Hey, I'm Nicky. Who are you? No really, who *are* you? Not your name or title. Who are you?

Take a step back, take a deep breath, and shout out something, anything you think of first, really loudly! What did you say? Please know that there is no correct or incorrect answer, but just out of curiosity, did you say what you think that you should have said... perhaps not truly what you wanted to say? Or did you truly say what you wanted to?

I'll share — here's mine.

My name is Nicky. <u>I AM</u> in control of what I can control. <u>I AM</u> an immigrant. I was born in the UK and I became a Canadian resident in 2013 — a huge challenge that <u>I AM</u> proud to say that I accomplished. <u>I AM</u> successful as a fitness professional influencing on a global scale. <u>I AM</u> a mum, a wife, a sister, a daughter, and a granddaughter. <u>I AM</u> an author. <u>I AM</u> anything that I want to be. <u>I AM</u> in control of my own actions.

Let me expand a little more on this exercise, its context, and why I have included it in this chapter.

In the summer of 2018, my daughter was 18 months old and ready to head off to daycare. I was shit scared. Not for her, oh no. I knew that she would be fine. She craves socialization, conversation, and interaction with children and adults. I was shit scared for ME. Who am I if I am not Mum? Does that make me Nicky, wife, sister…or am I just me? Just me? Yuck, why is that so demeaning? Who the heck was I, and why do I hate the thought of being me?

I tried the exercise that I just gave you a few times, and I honestly could not come up with anything else apart from adjectives that only described my feelings. <u>I AM</u> tired, angry, short-tempered, frustrated, and tired. Wait, did I say tired already? This was not great. Seriously, why was I having such an issue distancing and identifying myself away from being "Mum?" Why was there nothing at the end of my <u>I AM</u> statement that remotely sounded like an affirmation?

At first, I saw this as a small issue. Well, what do you expect? You have been a full-time Mum for 18 months. It's normal, it's natural. No biggie. Then it started to really burn in the back of my brain. Yeah, sure, in a practical sense I am a Mother. That's correct; I now have a baby. But here's the thing that I just couldn't shake: being a Mother is not all that I am. I am not a subservient human here purely for the need of another. Why do I not have anything positive to say about myself?

For weeks I was emotional, with random outbursts of tears, not interested in working out, food, sex, or even conversation with friends. I did not know why. My husband stirred up an idea to sit down alone in the quiet of the house and just write — put pen to paper and see what came out. Could I answer the question, *Who am I?* At first I was like, *say what now?* But after sleeping on it I thought, well why not? Perhaps it may help me better identify what the heck was going on, and maybe, just maybe, (and most importantly) make me feel a whole heap better and not be ashamed of just being me.

The next day I did just that. Pen to paper with no distractions, I sat down and wrote. I wept and wrote. Tears and snot dripped all over the paper and I wrote down the following: *I have no idea who I am. Did the world move on without me? I am not good enough to return to the fitness industry. I am 20lbs overweight and I feel like shit.* I think you get the idea of the thought process by now. Negative thoughts. Disbelief that I could be anything other than an overweight, unfit, frumpy Mum.

By the end of the writing session — which was quick and intense because once those flood gates opened, it all came out — I felt this immediate sense of relief. It was as if I had verbally vomited all the crap out. Seeing it on the paper and getting it all out, rather than it all being stuck in my head, was liberating. It also helped to see what self-talk was going on inside.

It was somewhat clear after that writing session. I had lost my identity aside from being "Mum." I had also lost my confidence in being anything else other than a Mum. I was also terrified. Who the heck am I? Can I even achieve an affirmation, an 'I AM' statement? This then stirred up a whole new conversation, which unfortunately turned out to be not so healthy or beneficial. Let me explain.

After my writing exercise epiphany, it seemed obvious. I can just return back to who I was before my daughter. Easy! I can make all of this happen by next week. Quick fix! I will get back on the schedule and teach a fitness class, take a cycle class or two, and eat only 1000 calories per day (Fact: you need over 1800 per day to sustain breastfeeding). I can lose 20lbs in like one week... right?! I can claim the old me back and kick ass! It will be just like it was before.

WRONG! My body has been through trauma. It needs to heal. Nothing is going to change in one week! I had unrealistic goals and an equally unrealistic time frame. The downward spiral of those naive expectations and goals hit me hard, like a sack of potatoes. It is like going back to an ex. You remember all the good times. You see through rose-tinted glasses. All was peachy, but when you're honest and you take off those glasses, it really was kinda shitty, and that's why you broke up in the first place.

I quite clearly needed help. I needed to be brave and ask for help — real professional help.

To seriously make change I needed to create change. We are not what we think. We are what we do. I could sit here all day and talk about what I needed to do, but what it comes down to is: I needed to turn my thoughts and self-discovery findings into action. I needed to take the first step. I called my family doctor, and she arranged for me to see a social worker.

Then I did what I am pretty sure the average person does after they book their first appointment to see a professional about their mental health. I put the phone down and said, "This is crazy. This is stupid. There is nothing wrong with me." This is an early sign of poor mental health.

Here are some other signs:

- *Feeling disconnected*
- *Illogical thinking*
- *Nervousness*
- *Unusual behaviour*
- *Problems thinking or concentrating*
- *Sleep or appetite changes*
- *Withdrawal*

So yeah, I needed to see a mental health expert!

It's weird to sit in a room with a person you have never met before and talk about yourself. The room was dimly lit with lamps. It was a small but comfortable space, and no, I did not lie down on a sofa with my head on a small cushion like in the movies! I just sat in a chair; a regular, plastic chair.

We actually started with a breathing exercise. That was nice. It broke the ice and calmed me down. From there, there were a series of questions, and then I had an opportunity to ask questions, too. I had time to speak if I wanted to, and time to be quiet. She called me on my BS and it was surprising at first, but cathartic at the same time. I enjoyed that there was no "lip service."

After seeing my social worker for a few weeks, a change was beginning to occur. Instead of running away — both physically and mentally — I stopped, held my space, and started to breathe. *Really breathe.* I breathed with my body and mind. Sometimes I closed my eyes. <u>I AM</u> in control of what I can control. Whoa! My first <u>I AM</u> statement. My first affirmation!

One step at a time, I began to really take control of what I could. It started small with my breath, and then manifested into more. I took joy in the little wins along the way, like having a shower when I wanted to and not just when I could. I felt sexy, strong, and proud of myself. I had come a long way since my emotional writing session. Before too long my visits with my social worker became less frequent, until they stopped completely. This was roughly a 6-month time period.

As I became more confident and started taking control of what I could, I noticed that the change in me was having a direct impact on my daughter. My demeanor, choice of words, vocal tone, and body language was for the positive. Our interactions became more energetic, fun, and patient. She was looking for guidance as she developed and grew, too. We started to vibe. She was learning from me and I was learning from her.

I claimed my space back on the fitness podium and I owned it, not just for me but as a role model for my daughter and a matriarch for all other mamas out there. I kicked ass as I embraced my new "mom bod" — and celebrated it. Sure, it will never be the same as before, but why would I want to go backward, anyway? Moving forward with this body that created life, and embracing it, allowed my hormonal balance to regulate, my mindset to be free, and all chains of expectation were released. I lost weight without being fixated on it. I purposely set my attention on becoming stronger and more fit through mindful, functional movement. That is how I could best serve myself and be a physical role model for my daughter. In all honesty, I prefer my physical appearance now, compared to pre-baby.

For the first time in a long time, I feel that I have an identity. My full journey from the start of this story until where I am today, writing this, is a time period of three years. Please do not let that time frame intimidate or dishearten you. What is important to remember is that it is your journey, and it will take you as long as it takes. Know that there are some wonderful learning opportunities along the way. I am grateful that it took some time to get here.

Being "Mum" is fantastic. Being "me" and a Mum is even better! I AM proud of who I am, and now I celebrate the challenging and agonizing journey. Taking care of oneself is the first step in being able to care for and inspire others.

Be iN iT wiTH THeM. THey aRe LeaRNiNG HOW to DO THiS GiG Too!

Being a parent is hard, but easy at the same time. I have never been so tired but so alive! Parenting is full of oxymorons. I started to make peace with this over time. I control what I can, and let go of what I cannot. Learn from mistakes. Fall down and get back up again. If you colour outside of the lines, be more careful next time. Walk before you can run. These are all comments and advice that we say and give to our children, but why oh why do we not take our own advice? Ease up on the pressure, Mama, and be in it with them. They are learning how to do this gig just like you. Learn together and make mistakes together. You will bond. You will vibe. You will also argue and get frustrated with each other, but all in all, you will become best buds.

My daughter is now three. I thought I was tired when I had a newborn…Haha! I had no idea. If you have a "threenager" or have experienced one, you know exactly what I am talking about! I am exhausted, but I bloody love it.

Every day she challenges me to be the best version of myself, because that is what she deserves: the very best of me. In turn, I challenge her to be the best version of herself, because that is what she deserves. Yes, you read that correctly. Go back and read that again. In other words: you need to be the best version of you so that she can be the best version of herself. Anything less does not do her justice. She should be every inch of her perfect self, empowered and full of self-belief. As I mentioned in part one, you need to find yourself before you can begin to care for and inspire others.

Let's get back to parenting. I realised pretty quickly that trying to put the stereotypical parenting theories into action — like *do as you are told* and *because I said so* — was not going to cut it. If I am honest, that style is just plain ass lazy. As a kid growing up in the 80s in England, that was parenting, so it makes sense that it became my default style. But things were different then (and I am not just talking about how there were no computers and how the internet was not accessible yet)! I am talking about the fact that it was ok to spank your child. I even got the chalk board eraser thrown at me by a teacher at school, and that was deemed okay!

We are more educated now about children's mental response and development. We speak freely and easily now about topics that were taboo in the 80s, so it was no big surprise that my 80s-style of parenting wasn't working. Anyway, *because I said so* is just horseshit. That is not parenting; that is being a dictator.

Once my husband and I really started to "parent" past the baby months of just eat, sleep, and poop (roughly around the age of 10 months), we decided to converse with our daughter as if she were a mini version of ourselves. We spoke to her as we would like to be spoken to and listened to her like we would like to be heard. We talked with her as a tiny human, not a baby. No "goo-goo-ga-ga," but real words and real conversations. Staying away from baby talk helped us immensely in building better communication from an early age. As we led by example using the correct words, our daughter's vocabulary grew quickly. This reduced friction, as conversations could be held, resulting in better understanding of what was needed or being communicated. You know what that equals? Less tantrums! Yay!

Hey, here's a story from my experience as an example of being *in it* with them as they learn.

It is a regular challenge to get our daughter to put on her shoes. Remember that my default parenting response is usually, at full volume, "Just put on your shoes, come on!" But, in all honesty, if you shouted at me to put my shoes on I would probably just go slower or throw the shoes at you. Boom! That was exactly my daughter's response. So yeah…*eye roll*

This rephrasing of the same sentence worked like a charm for our daughter, "It's time to get your shoes on. Which shoes would you like to wear today to match your outfit?" It worked for her — and actually, if you said that to me, it would make me want to select a great pair of shoes and put them on to check out if they went with my outfit. I gave her the power to choose, the ability to make decisions, rather than taking that away from her by asking her to just do as she is told. Now she is in control and I can just step back and commend her on a great job. Way better vibes! Now, don't get me wrong, I still shout and wail like a banshee and have to reel myself in regularly, take a breath, rephrase, and, where possible, try to consider how I would like to be asked to do something. How would *I* like to receive feedback? How would *I* feel because of this situation I have been placed in?

Your kid truly is your mini-me, regardless if it is you or your partner doing the "parenting." Your kids are little replicas of you. What they see, hear, and feel is a direct result of what we put out there. They are also watching and listening all of the time (even when you don't know it)! I found out the hard way one summer's day last year when my daughter said to me, "I am going to get that fucking fly" as she swung the fly swatter around the kitchen.

Momming is hard. Dadding is hard. Parenting is hard. Losing weight is hard. Eating healthy is hard. Saving money is hard. There is no correct way or perfect way to complete those tasks, so ease up on trying to be a perfect, mama. What does "perfect" even mean, anyway?

We try to match the "perfect" that everyone else believes and what we think they should see, when, truly, the only "perfect" we should care about is our own interpretation of that word. So, hey, take a moment and jot down what perfect parenting looks like, feels like, and sounds like to you.

_____

_____

_____

_____

_____

_____

Whatever you have written above is perfect parenting for you.

In Summary

That very first moment that you become a Mum and hold your baby for the first time is overwhelming. You do not know where to start. You have read every book, asked your friends and family, and searched the internet, and they all have conflicting messages. Momming is hard and easy, fun and frustrating, and no two experiences are the same.

Educate yourself, create a strong support network, and trust your instincts. It will all fall into place — and if you get it wrong today, tomorrow you will get it right.

Look after yourself. I have written this sentence three times in my chapter because it is that important. *Taking care of oneself is the first step in being able to care for and inspire others.*

Learn from your children just as they learn from you. Be humble, patient, and kind. Be silly and engaged in each moment. The days are long, but the years are short.

Enjoy this wild ride, Mama. You've got this.

CHAPTER 17

Barbara Parker

FIND BARBARA: **@MOMBSHELL.BARBS**

Back in January of 1996, a little girl entered the world. She was given an antique name, Barbara, after her late great-grandmother, but because it's an older name and not heard much (especially to someone in their twenties), nobody ever knew how to spell it correctly. In the fitting rooms or at a restaurant, the host taking names for the waiting list would often say, "Barbara???? That's an old name, huh?" or "Barbara doesn't really suit you; you're too young." That little girl would go on for years and years hating her name, sometimes using her middle name instead just to make it easier. Well, that girl is me, and I am happy to report that I no longer hate my name! I've actually really grown to love my name and feel honoured to be given this name. It's different and unique, and I like to think of myself in the same way — different and unique!

But the name that I hear a thousand times a day is most definitely "Mommy" — Mommy this, Mommy that — and I finally understand why my mom always said that she wanted to change her name! Lol. A few other names used to get my attention are: Barb, Barbs, or my personal favourite, Mombshell (there's a whole story behind "Mombshell," but I'll have to save that one for a later date).

I am 25 years old. My son is four, and he is also my best friend! We have a five-year-old blue-merle Aussie named Macey and a six-year-old fat, orange cat called Olaf (yes; he is named after the snowman in Frozen. His brother was Sven, but unfortunately, he passed when he was three). I am a photographer, and I have also recently become a big body positive/confident + self-love advocate through my social media platforms. I share my personal journey through self-discovery and self-love in hopes of inspiring other women, especially moms, to love themselves no matter their shape, weight, or size. Our physical attributes do NOT equal our worth! With that said, if you need a little body positive or self-love inspo, feel free to creep me @ mombshell.barbs on both Instagram and TikTok. (I'm kinda TikTok famous [hair flip]).

#momguilt is an area that I find myself still feeling a little insecure about at times. I question whether I'm doing a good enough job, or if I spend enough time with him. Am I feeding him enough healthy food? Is he watching too much TV? The list goes on and on. So, in this chapter, I'm going to be talking all about my own moments of #momguilt, because it's a subject that I don't hear being discussed often, if at all, especially in my online communities. #momguilt is very real. It can take a toll on you as a mother, and I'm 99.9% sure that every mom has experienced it at least once as a mother. So, let's start the conversation together!

For me, my first experience with mom guilt was before my son even came into this crazy-a** world. I had never been a mom at this point, so how the heck was I going to know if I'm doing it right or not? There are hundreds, if not thousands, of parenting books out there, and they all contain different (and sometimes contradictory) stories and advice. I think these books can make the worrying worse, because now I've set standards for myself as a parent — just to match another person's version of what parenting looks like for them.

With all of this conflicting information out there, it definitely just made me worry more. I worried if I would even be a good mom in the first place. Is he getting enough nutrients from me to be able to grow for those long nine months inside of me? I worried about whether I would be able to handle the hard days while keeping my cool, because I know that I can be...passionate. I also worried if I would have that natural "mothers' instinct" to wake up when he started fussing in the night. I'm a sleep-as-deep-as-a-bear-in-hibernation kinda girl. Honestly, a robber could probably take everything in the house, including the pillow right from under my head, and I probably wouldn't wake up.

I also felt like I had to buy all of the baby things: the swings, bouncy chairs, jolly jumpers, exersaucers, and pretty much anything baby-related. But now I understand why I — and I'm sure most other moms — have these same kinds of questions, worries, and guilt. We truly just want to give our babies the world and so much more, which makes us put so much pressure on ourselves to try and be the perfect parent. The thing is...the "perfect parent" does not exist. There is no one-size-fits-all style of parenting, and I can promise you, you're going to make mistakes. I swear it's like a rite of passage into motherhood!

I have wanted to be a mom for as long as I can remember. I have two younger siblings with a seven and eight year age gap between me, which meant that I got to help with changing their diapers (because apparently, at seven years old, it's a fun thing to do?). I just always really enjoyed being around children. Watching how their little minds develop over time has to be one of the coolest things to observe.

So, when I was 18, I got my first full-time job as a nanny. I nannied for four years, between three different families. As a nanny, you truly get to grow a beautiful bond with the children — considering you're with them for a large portion of their day, it would be hard not to. It was also interesting to see how different the children were with their parents around and without, and I also got to observe multiple parenting styles. With that I built an image of how I imagined my-self as a mom. I imagined the things that I would do as a parent, and the things that I might try to avoid — but I knew that each decision would be of my own preference, not just what I saw other moms doing.

During my four years as a nanny, there were a lot of different life events that happened in that time. First off, I got married at the young age of 18 (I know what you're thinking, just wait for it...). Shortly after, my *then* husband (and there it is, LOL) was hired by the Canadian Armed Forces and we were eventually posted to Trenton, where we moved an hour east to the air force base. After moving out there, we got two kittens, then a puppy, and then we bought a house! Shortly after we signed the papers for our new home, we got the great news that we were preggers, with an expected arrival date of October 29, 2016 (November 1st works, too).

As I grew my sweet baby inside of me for nine months, I dreamt of the moment that I would finally get to hold him or her in my arms. Would I have a boy or girl? I would imagine the newborn days, skin-to-skin contact, and rocking my baby to sleep. Mostly, though, I was really looking forward to breastfeeding. I had a few moments of wondering if I'd be able to do it. Could I handle the pain I had heard so much about? I really wanted to feel that "bond" I had always heard being discussed around breastfeeding. It makes sense — they're literally attached to your boob for the majority of their newborn stage. You're solely in charge of providing your baby with all of the nutrients they need. But what if I couldn't breastfeed? What if he didn't latch? Would I still have that deep connection and bond with my baby?

Unfortunately, this became my reality, and I found myself asking these same questions that I had been worried about. The reason I was unable to breastfeed was because I ended up being hospitalized just four days after delivering (I'll touch a little more on that further in the chapter). I really feared I wouldn't get that bond. When I was finally out of the hospital, I knew I didn't have that bond with him yet, but I also knew that I didn't really have the opportunity to do so due to being so sick.

So here is this beautiful baby boy that I just grew inside of me, where my heartbeat literally made his heart beat, yet somehow he didn't feel like my baby. I wasn't sure exactly why I was sort of resenting my sweet and innocent baby. I felt absolutely awful and like the worst mom ever because I wasn't obsessed with my baby. Was it from being in the hospital for so long? Had I lost the window to bond? Was it from not breastfeeding due to being sick? Or maybe it was because I wasn't able to rock him and sing lullabies to him for his first couple months of life?

The #momguilt started to really set in and became a pretty heavy weight to carry, but I was too embarrassed to tell anyone. Imagine being a new mom, telling someone that you didn't really care to hold your baby. So instead, I just suffered in silence. I suffered through it on my own, when I didn't have to.

As time passed and I started getting back to myself, that's when I finally got my bond with him. I was worried for so long, for no reason. I know that my friends and family would have supported me 100% had I asked for help, instead of feeling too embarrassed and guilty for feeling my human feelings. So don't be afraid to ask for help. All that matters is that you are getting better. If you don't have close friends or family to help, there are tons of amazing online communities full of moms ready to help another mom.

The next experience with mom guilt came not too long after Emerson was born. I knew that the first couple of days would be hard with a newborn, and being first-time parents added to that difficulty. But by day two, I started to have a lot of pain in my abdomen (story time).

I started to have trouble getting up and down on my own. My mom and I both asked the nurses for stronger pain medication multiple times because the Tylenol and Advil they were providing weren't helping. My mom said something wasn't right. Actually, it was more around the lines of, "I've had three children, Barbara, and I was never in that much pain or had trouble moving around." But the nurses assured me that I was okay and that I just needed to rest some more. They're the professionals. They do this every day. They know what they're doing...or so I thought.

We were discharged three days postpartum, and I was still in the most amount of pain I think I have ever felt in my life. I also didn't want to go back to the hospital because now wherever I went the baby went, because I was breastfeeding. The second night home around 11:00 p.m., I told my (then) husband to call an ambulance because I couldn't move and could hardly lift my head up. I was rushed by ambulance to Trenton hospital, where they were calling Belleville because they were sending me to the ICU, as they would be more equipped to help me. Although I was in a lot of pain, I didn't really feel scared because I didn't know what was happening. All I knew was that I was in excruciating pain. I never once thought death was a possibility! I was in (but didn't know this at the time) septic shock, sepsis, and respiratory failure — on the verge of cardiac arrest. I was rushed to Belleville hospital ICU where they told me that they were putting me to sleep so they could put a tube down my throat to help me breathe, which I very much needed.

I woke up thirteen days later. I was now in Kingston hospital, where I was told I had been airlifted to. Along with that, I was then told that I had unfortunately lost my uterus, both fallopian tubes, and one ovary, all destroyed by the infection that literally nearly killed me, called Group A Streptococcus.

My recovery was long and hard. I had to rebuild all of my strength and muscle back. When I first woke up, just holding my phone felt like I was holding a brick, and I couldn't lift my own head. I was so weak. I stayed in the hospital for another almost two weeks. Upon being released, I was told I still had to have two people to help me walk, one on each side, but the worst was when they told my family to not let me carry my own baby until I was completely stable on my own. I totally understand why, but it was really shitty being told by someone else that I couldn't do something with MY baby.

At this point I had no independence. I needed help to do pretty much everything, so I knew I wasn't capable of taking care of a baby. I didn't get to do all of the new mom things like breastfeeding, getting peed on when changing their diaper, rocking them when they cried, holding them all day just because. Instead, I had to watch others take care of my baby. Then, I didn't even want to hold him while sitting, and I couldn't tolerate hearing his cries. If I was holding him when he started to cry, my heart would just start racing because I knew I was unable to soothe him, so I would quickly have to pass him off to someone that was able to.

Having to watch someone else be able to get up and rock your baby while they cry felt like absolute shit! I didn't feel like his mom — or a mom at all. In my head I had already failed as a mother because I didn't get to breastfeed him like I had planned (although I do know #fedisbest, and I am very thankful that there was an alternative for him when I was unable to provide). I didn't get to bathe him, burp him, or change him. I felt useless and defeated. This was not what I had imagined life being like after having him, and it never crossed my mind that I wouldn't get to do all of the newborn things with him.

The whole time I was thinking that I'm just a terrible mom — the worst mom — but Emerson only had love for me. He wasn't the one blaming me for not being able to breastfeed, or change his diaper — that was all me! The #momguilt was getting so bad that I started to think that my baby wasn't going to like me. I accepted that he'd be a Daddy's boy. That guilt took a little while to get past, but once I was fully healed, I felt like I finally got to be a Mom and I could really start to bond with him. It felt amazing. I fell completely in love with my sweet baby boy. Then, all of a sudden, I was just OBSESSED with him! Although I still have days where I feel a bit of guilt for missing so much of the beginning of his life, I just remind myself of the incredible bond that we have now. I remind myself that he doesn't even know what happened in those first few weeks, and he will never remember it.

Finally, the #momguilt that I struggle the most with these days is his father and my divorce. When I was pregnant, I never dreamed that divorce might be in my future. I was married, had a house, a baby, and a dog; I thought I knew what the rest of my life was going to look like. We talked about how many children we wanted, places we wanted to travel to, and the things we would do when we retired.

The universe has a weird way of working. Unfortunately, I came to realize that the life I thought I had all planned and figured out was no longer what I envisioned for my future. It was an extremely hard decision to leave his father, but it was a necessary decision not just for myself, but for all of us. I have found that parents who stay together just for the kids end up completely resenting each other. I couldn't be that same good wife anymore, and I didn't want Emerson to grow up in a home filled with negative energy, because I know that's where it would have gone.

It was just before his second birthday that we officially split, and I moved back to our hometown to be close to my friends and family. I knew I would need their support. I also knew that it was going to be hard, but it has been so much harder than I thought it would be. The list goes on for that, but watching your child go through the confusion and the emotions from all the changes was — and still is — the worst and absolutely most heart-wrenching feeling. So, my #momguilt is on a lot lately, but I just keep doing my absolute best to be the best mom in guiding him through these times and making sure that he knows that he has so much support. Although it is a hard and massive change, I have to remind myself of why I made that decision, and that I am not a terrible mom for it.

#momguilt is real. We all feel it at one point or another, but please remember that those thoughts and feelings only come from us placing that guilt there. Remembering that you are never alone is so important. Whatever it is you are feeling #momguilt over, I promise you that another mom is feeling that same way, too. So let's start normalizing talking about our #momguilt and continuing to grow an incredible community of moms helping other moms. Don't be afraid to ask for help, advice, or even to just share your story — because there is at least one mom out there who will be able to relate.

CHAPTER 18

Sarah Power Smith

FIND SARAH: **@SARAHPOWERSMITH**

L ife is going to throw stuff at you when you least expect it. This I can promise you. Sometimes the stuff is off-the-charts amazing, and sometimes it's the shittiest of the shitty. I'm realizing that this is just how life works. It's the whole yin-yang thing, friends. The irony of it all is that it's the moments that bring us to our knees that end up feeding our strength. The challenges we face in life are what propel our confidence and our desire to persevere. They remind us that we can do hard things, so we proudly place our feet firmly on the earth below and move one foot in front of the other.

My name is Sarah. I am a Registered Massage Therapist and I have a background in Nursing. 90s hip hop makes me happy and I'm a massive lover of pizza! I am a mother to four incredible kids. I am a widow.

My husband and I met and began dating when I was 16 and he was 19. My parents were less than thrilled that I was seeing someone who could legally drink, but didn't so much mind him taking on the role as my new chauffeur, carting my ass around in his shiny new tan Pontiac Sunfire. Our existence was filled with cottage weekends lakeside and hanging out with friends. We finished up our post secondary education. I became an RN and then decided to avoid adulthood a little longer by becoming a Massage Therapist. We were married after dating for eight years and, soon after, he became a firefighter. I popped out four kids over the next eight years. Our existence was filled with diapers and lacrosse games. Life was busy. Life was good!

Four years ago, Jeff was diagnosed with stage 4 colon cancer. He passed away one year later, leaving behind myself and our four children, ages 15, 11, 8, and 6.

In the very beginning I was sure it was appendicitis. He had a mild ache in his right side that had lasted about three days. I clutched to my knowledge as a nurse and was sure that appendicitis was the most reasonable explanation. Jeff went to the hospital to have it checked, just as a precaution, while I dragged the kids to my oldest son's lacrosse playoff game. I remember his text like it was yesterday: "Omg. I just heard the 'C' word."

When we were first told that he had cancer, I remember saying "no big deal! This is just a bump in the road!" For weeks that saying was my go-to. After all, he had no previous signs or symptoms! I was positive we'd be told it was caught early. He'd have surgery, then chemo, and we'd continue on with our lives, ever so grateful for the shake up and reset. We would be so appreciative to have been reminded of what is truly important, and we would flourish!

Um, yeah. That's not exactly how things went. Months of seeing specialists and genetic testing resulted in us being told that Jeff's cancer was a particularly aggressive form. When we eventually found out that his cancer was incurable, my saying changed to "as long as the kids are okay, I'll be okay." My focus pivoted to being his full-time caregiver and supporting the emotional wellbeing of our four kids. In all honesty, I felt like my needs didn't matter. Jeff and the kids were my full and complete focus.

When Jeff passed away, I clung tightly to my mantra and very intentionally avoided taking care of myself. After all, looking at where I was hurting was counterproductive, right? I wanted to feel better, not worse! I was tired of feeling sad, and honestly I didn't have the capacity to do the deep work. I was so worried that if I let myself completely break down and feel all the feels, that I might not be able to climb back to "normal." I kept those protective walls up nice and high. It was a very real and legit fear of mine.

Two-and-a-half weeks after Jeff passed, the kids started back to school. The first day of school was always a day that Jeff and I were both present for. It was important to us that we see the kids off together. Beginning a new school year without him present was tough and emotional, but it was a great distraction for our now crew of five. After drop off, a few close friends and I went for breakfast. As we sipped our coffee and replayed the morning, our waitress came by, eager to take our order. "I'll have two eggs, homefries, and toast, please." I politely asked. When she questioned me on how I wanted my eggs, I froze. *How did I want my eggs? I wanted my eggs however Jeff usually ordered my eggs!* I thought. And there it was. The very first moment of many where I realized just how much I let my late husband make decisions for me. It was completely and utterly unnerving. Like, what in the actual fuck? How did I not have an answer for such a simple question? How did I get to this place?

As the months passed, I began to struggle more and more. I was so relieved that my kids were working through their stuff and were pretty happy humans for the most part, but it became abundantly clear that there were a lot of areas that I was avoiding — both healing from and growing from. As much as I was fighting it, it was time to shake things up and put myself on the front burner. The back burner no longer felt like home.

Six months after Jeff died I began to see a therapist. It was one of the best decisions I made at the time, hands down! Not only did I begin to face my grief and process my feelings around my husband's illness and death, but I slowly began to notice all of the times in my life that I did not make myself a priority. I started to recognize all of the areas that I had let my husband take control of, setting boundaries for the both of us and making most of the decisions — big and small. Don't get me wrong, I was totally cool with it for the most part. I mean, think about it. It took the pressure off of me to make the "right" decisions (aka zero repercussions comin' my way). Everyone liked me because I was the "good guy." I wasn't the one making anyone feel uncomfortable by enforcing rules or setting boundaries. Letting Jeff dictate things in our life allowed me to stay nice and safe and comfy. I was the mediator. I was the people pleaser that everyone liked.

There's just one massive problem with this. The "play it safe good guy" worked for me when my husband was by my side, but not so much after transitioning to solo life. I suddenly felt as if I was left defenseless in a very big, open world. I felt shaky about making decisions. I wasn't clear on my likes and dislikes, and I had NO CLUE what a boundary was, let alone how to set one. I was very unexpectedly faced with having to make a big shift and take on roles that were insanely unfamiliar to me. Nobody told me this shit when he was sick. I felt as if I was floating, completely untethered. I felt like a fish out of water.

Of course, I anticipated being devastated. I expected to feel overwhelmed with funeral arrangements and paperwork and the difficult task of packing my husband's clothes up in our closet. I expected to feel the heaviness of supporting my kids and the craziness of five separate grief counselling sessions a week. I prepared myself for feeling lonely even though I would be constantly surrounded by my loving family and supportive friends. I even anticipated the financial stress that was to come. What I did NOT expect was the extreme shift in dynamics in my life and home as a result of the changes in roles I would face. I became it all. Mom, Dad, financial decision maker, scraped knee kisser, lacrosse expert, life scheduler, homework enforcer, in-law communicator, and advocate of all important things.

One of the biggest shifts in parenting was becoming the "bad guy." I was completely unaware of how much I relied on my partner to be the disciplinarian in our family — until he was gone, that is. It's funny how out of control you feel when you can no longer yell "everybody better finish their homework/tidy their rooms/finish their chores/get into bed because Daddy will be home ANY MINUTE!" My kids now had to do these things, not for fear of consequences from their father, but simply because I was asking them to. Was it challenging? You bet your ass it was. Were there tears? Yelling? Locking myself in the bathroom? Yup. There were entire counselling sessions dedicated to my new and challenging roles.

I will admit that for the first few months I wallowed in anger and frustration. Anger towards Jeff for leaving me. Anger that I had to be all of the things now. Anger that every damn responsibility and decision was on me and me alone. I even felt anger and guilt that I was angry, because I told myself that I should just be thankful that I was the one alive. Everything felt unfair and nothing felt normal.

After weeks, months, and years of counselling, journaling, talking to friends, leaning on family, making mistakes, reflecting, learning to communicate better, and a whole lot of trial and error, I can finally say that I feel more like myself than I ever have. Actually, that's not completely true. I have far surpassed my expectation of who I thought I could be. Losing Jeff has forced me to grow and evolve in ways I could not have imagined, as odd as that feels to say. Grief has made me a better person.

The relationships in my life have become stronger, and I am a better friend. I know what true friendship looks like because I was shown it by my closest friends when I needed them the most. I value those relationships deeply, and have learned to let go of other relationships that were not serving me. I am a better mother, and I feel a closeness to my children that I never imagined possible. Losing their father has deeply bonded us and has allowed us all a new perspective. Yes, they still fight, and yes, it's a shit show sometimes (just for the record). I don't necessarily parent the way Jeff did, but it's my way and it works for us.

Grief has compelled me to be far more on top of and organized with my finances. With all of the responsibility now on me, I made it a priority to manage my budget and educate myself on preparing for my future, rather than burying my head.

I am healthier today than I have ever been. I want to live a long, full life, and to be active in my children's lives. Watching your partner's health deteriorate makes you realize how important it is to look after your own health. No more being inactive. No more bypassing regular checkups. Not anymore.

I know without a doubt that losing my husband was one of the hardest things that I will ever have to go through. At times I felt like I couldn't breathe, and now it's the memories of all of those hard moments that feed my strength. I am strong because I know that I have it in me to cope with the most shattering situations. I have confidence because I've proven to myself that I can actually do this life on my own, with my feet firmly planted on the earth below; day after day, moving one foot in front of the other.

CHAPTER 19

Darci Prince

FIND DARCI: **@DARCIIPRINCE**

I may answer to "Mama" at home every day, but I still don't feel worthy of the title. I mean, I still call my mom for things, so there is no way that I am actually a mom! I just changed lightbulbs for the first time in my life. I don't own a snow shovel. I live off of coffee, Fizz Sticks, and dry shampoo. I don't know how to change a tire on my car, and yet I'm somehow responsible for keeping a tiny human alive. It blows my mind how we're required to take part in so much training to work a job or drive a car, and yet we birth a human being and a few days later (or sometimes the same day) we're allowed to just walk out of the hospital with it! What in the actual hell is that about? Where is the training manual for that?

I'm Darci Prince, and I'm responsible for keeping a two-year-old little boy alive on the daily. His name is Grayson and he is the brightest
spot in my life — but he has also been one of the sources of some
dark spots as well. I'm going to be straight with you here — I had a
rough pregnancy, a tough recovery after Grayson made his arrival,
and I struggled with postpartum depression on my maternity leave.
Becoming a mom took some adjusting for me because I had never felt "baby fever" and there was no void that I felt needed to be
filled by this little being. Please understand, I LOVE MY LITTLE
HUMAN! He is so smart, adorable, and absolutely hilarious. He
makes me laugh every single day. But hot damn, it has been a tough
road. This shit is hard. And even though everyone says, "it'll get
easier"…well, I'm still waiting.

I've always been afraid to say these things to those who don't have
kids yet, are soon-to-be-moms, or are new moms, because I don't
want them to think that it's all horrible; it's not! But it's also not all
butterflies and rainbows that are commonly shown on social media.
I think it's important to know that if and when you aren't glowing
and madly in love with your human every second of every day, IT
IS OKAY!

I present to you my dirty laundry — my struggles with mental
health, managing our own expectations, and being a working mom,
real and in print for all to read!

Imagine that you've recently broken your arm and it's in a sling. You
have to go get groceries so you head to the store with your toddler to
do the shopping. You get your items, the packer fills up the cart with
your bags, and you make your way to the car. On your way out of
the store, while you're pushing the cart with your toddler in the seat
and a cart full of items, your child starts screaming. They decide to
have a temper tantrum (for any given reason) at that very moment.
You have one good arm, trying to get the child into their car seat,
knowing full well that you still must load up the bags of food into

your car. In this scenario, it is likely that someone would see your struggle and offer you some assistance. From the outside, it looks like you are struggling. It appears that you are likely in pain and could use some assistance. They would likely load up your groceries for you so that you can take care of your child.

That's what physical injuries do. They show people that you are not at your best in that moment and that you need a helping hand.

But what about a mental illness? What about invisible illnesses in general? Things like concussions, anxiety, depression, post-traumatic stress disorder, obsessive compulsive disorder, or addiction? Things that go on inside of our brains or that we live with every single day, but no one can necessarily *see* that we're struggling with. Why not? Well, because you *look* like you're fine. No one jumps in to help you when you're trying to deal with a crying baby. You just have to deal with it on your own; you look like you're capable. You look like you *should* be able to do it. So, no one offers to help. If anything, others see you and give a sympathetic nod or smile and it's a little bit amusing, because, well, we've all been there! Meanwhile, you want to be the one crying and screaming and flailing on the floor because you can't handle it anymore — because that is how your *every day* feels.

No one knows that, however. No one knows what's going on inside your mind. No one knows that it's been three days since you've brushed your teeth or had a shower because you don't have the energy or willpower to do so. No one knows that it is taking everything in you to just put some kind of clothes on that day. No one knows that you're consistently napping when the child is napping. And it isn't because you're lazy, but because you *need* that nap in order to function for the rest of the day. No one knows that the reason why you don't prepare home-cooked meals isn't because you're a bad cook. It's because you have so many other thoughts playing pinball in your brain all day, every day that you forget to eat, let alone prepare food for the others in your household. This is what you're dealing with every single day.

You can't stop parenting and you can't turn off your mental illness. You have no choice but to learn how to live with both. It's important to find out how to balance your illness and your parenting so that you can manage. You don't need to be great at both. You don't need to be a superhero, but you do need to manage. Seek help, gather resources, and build up your personal toolbox of ways to help you cope so that your day-to-day is manageable and neither you nor your family gets neglected. Your mental health is vitally important; balance is everything.

Another thing that we, as moms, need to learn to balance and manage is the unrealistic standards that we set for ourselves (and our families).

As parents, we often hear that we need to stop comparing ourselves to what we see on social media. It is important to live our lives and raise our children the way we feel is right, and not how Pinterest dictates that we should. But those aren't the standards or expectations that I'm referring to here. I'm talking about the expectations that we set up for ourselves. We set the bar so high for ourselves and the things that we want so badly that we try to control every moment of every event in our child's life.

I'm talking about how we envision all of the "firsts" happening. How every "first" event is going to take place, and all of the cute pictures that will be taken. Learning how to accept the realities of what actually takes place — the screaming and crying that actually happened or the missed photos and the family events that came and went without any photos at all — takes serious willpower. The events that I'm referring to include (but are not limited to): the first birthday, the first holidays (Easter, Thanksgiving, Christmas, Mother's and Father's Day, etc.), Baptism (if applicable), first celebration or party for the appropriate sporting event (Superbowl/World Series/Stanley Cup), autumn photos at a pumpkin patch or apple orchard, or any other event or celebration that "should" have photos taken.

As I write this chapter I have been struggling with this myself over the last few months. My newsfeeds have been full of cutesy photos of families. I see photos of babies in adorable outfits, taking walks together in the autumn forests covered in red, yellow, and orange-coloured leaves. They are walking hand-in-hand while everyone is smiling, and no one seems to be having any temper tantrums. Meanwhile, in my household, my toddler is losing his mind because I won't let him eat crayons.

I want so badly to take him to one of these places, but I know that as soon as we do it will be nothing but a fight. We will pay the entrance fee, we will have to follow all of the new safety guidelines, my anxiety will likely flare up, I will be incredibly stressed, and I will have to work very, very hard just to get a cute photo. I understand that it's about more than just the photos. It's about the memories, but because this is all that I'm seeing on my timelines right now, I feel as though I have to make it happen. So, I have spent the last few weeks trying to rearrange the plans that were already set for my family and friends. I've been trying to find a time that we, as our little family, could go to one of these places so that I, too, could fabricate this happy autumn memory. How ridiculous is that?

Many of my child's firsts were complete write-offs. I've concluded that there are a few reasons as to why this happened: a) I set these standards too high for myself and for him; b) I expected them to go one way and then he's actually just a baby, so they completely did not go that way whatsoever; or c) other forces at play just did not want me to have any of the cutesy photos to commemorate the moments that everyone else seems to get.

Whatever it was, it seemed as though each of my son's firsts did not meet the expectations that I had set for myself. For example, in our family we have an Easter tradition called an egg fight; no, we do not throw eggs at one another. We decorate hard boiled eggs and tap one egg onto another. Whichever egg cracks is the loser. This continues until there is only one egg left standing — taadaa! They're the winner!

I have a photo of my grandpa helping me with my first egg fight when I was a baby, so naturally, I had this image in my mind that my dad would help my son with his first egg fight. It was going to be an adorable photo. In reality, Easter for my son did not go as planned. There were many people at our family gathering. The day got away from us, and not one photo was taken that day. So not only did the egg fight photo not happen, but I don't even actually have photos of my son at his first Easter.

Fast-forward to his first birthday. Good Lord, the first birthday. The custom cupcakes, the backdrop for the photos, the smash cake, the invitations, the food, the games, the goodie bags, the thank you gifts, the games for the kids, the giveaways for the kids, the activities to entertain the adults, the bubble machine, the ball pit, the photo ideas…SO MANY UNNECESSARY THINGS! And guess what, he was sick! He was lethargic, he had a fever, and he would not let go of me. I spent the entire three hours carrying around my child because he would not go to any of the 45 family members and friends that were there to see him for his first birthday. We took one family photo in front of the fancy backdrop that took me two-and-a-half hours to make, and that was it.

Why do we do this to ourselves? Why do we allow the external pressures of social media make us feel like we need to do these things, and why do we allow ourselves to feel like we're failing when they don't happen? Parenting is all about the unexpected. I used to work in event planning, where you have to expect that things are not going to go as planned. I used to do that for a living, and yet, for some reason, when it comes to my little human being I cannot seem to accept that things are not going to go as planned! We need to stop setting these ridiculous and unnecessary standards for ourselves and just accept that these little beings are going to do whatever they want to do.

And let's be honest: behind every cute photo that we see on our Instagram feeds or on our Facebook timelines, there are temper tantrums (also from moms and dads), there are tablets, singing parents, rattling toys, and treats being offered up in exchange for a cute smile or giggle to make that photo happen. For that one picture that is shared with a cheesy caption, there are 50 other photos on that cellphone that are of a screaming child who wants nothing to do with what the parents are trying to get them to do. Social media is a highlight reel. When you walk through someone's home and you see the pictures on the walls, that is a highlight reel. You cannot compare your every day to those moments. We do not post or print the photos of the unhappy moments.

With that said, keep this in mind, too. The photos that we want to frame — and the ones we want to post — are the ones that we want to use to remind ourselves that there are happy moments in and amongst all of these other disastrous days. Because although they are the highlight reel, they are moments too. The happy moments are there; we just have to remind ourselves of them when the tough times hit. But the truly happy moments that happen on their own and are not fabricated — those are the ones that you want to share and frame. Those make up the true highlight reel of your life. Enjoy the purely happy moments, the candid moments, and the real moments. And learn to go with the flow.

One final aspect of Momming that has been an ongoing challenge for me (thus far) is dealing with the guilt that comes with being a working mom. To stay at home or to go back to work, that is the question! For me, there was no doubt in my mind that I would be going back to work when my maternity leave was over. I applaud the women who can be full-time moms and stay at home with their kids, but that is not for me. It was never in my plans, and never became part of the plan once my son was born.

My work involves a busy environment where I have many tasks on the go at all times. I sit on multiple committees, and have events and projects constantly taking place. The adjustment from that life to being home, where my only responsibility was keeping my tiny human alive, really took a toll on me. Being a mom is part of who I am, but it is not ALL of who I am. I couldn't wait to be back in my work environment where I was accomplishing tangible tasks every day and making things happen.

When it came time to return to work, I had it in my head that my son would have his first birthday, he'd go to daycare, and off to work I'd go! In reality, I was not prepared for my return to work at all. I was especially unprepared for the onslaught of emotions that came when my incredible daycare provider would send photos and updates of how my son was doing each day. She'd send things like, "Today, we went for a walk and Grayson saw geese. Has he seen geese before? He was very intrigued. He was fixated on them the entire time!" Or, "Look who is taking more and more steps each time he gets up on those who wobbly legs of his!"

My lunch break would consist of looking at pictures with captions like, "Look, Mommy! I painted a picture and helped make cookies." I'd read the update of, "Grayson loved playing with his friends in the snow. They move around a lot easier than he does, but he enjoys himself. He also seemed to make out the word 'BLUE' today — hooray!"

While these photos and updates were the highlight of my day, they also broke my heart because I felt like I was missing out. In the grand scheme of things, I know these little moments (like seeing geese) are not life changing, but it is a first. I couldn't help but feel robbed of sharing that first moment with him.

When the world shut down here in the spring of 2020 with the Coronavirus, daycares closed and many work places closed as well. Due to the nature of my work, we were able to adapt to being remote so that I could continue to work from home. Our wonderful army of family (within our isolation bubble) rotated coming over and looking after Grayson while I worked. My office was set up in a back room which was attached to our basement living area. That area doubled as Grayson's play space.

This scenario hurt my heart and soul even more than when he was away at a daycare provider. I hated feeling this way when it was happening, and I still have a hard time thinking back to those feelings, but they deserve to be acknowledged. I hated that I was in the next room listening to Grayson giggle, full belly laugh, learn words and letters, colour, and play games with his Auntie, Nana, and Grandma while I was working. I am forever grateful to them that they were able to help us while I had to work. I *love* that they were making their own memories with him, and I love that they got to spend that time with him, but I couldn't help but feel so guilty that other people, even if they were *our* people, were raising my child.

You might be thinking, *well Darci, you want to work and you love your work, so you can't have it both ways* — and you're right. Working is important to me because it allows me to have a part of my life that is not directly tied to my little human; and I think that's critical to our wellbeing as moms. We need something that is OURS. Whether it's a hobby, a weekly hangout with our friends, a side hustle, a sports team, a job, or whatever it may be, we need something that is solely ours. Where I can be Darci and not *just* Grayson's mom. Work does that for me, and so does my side hustle.

But it is important to also acknowledge that we're allowed to feel what we feel. We're allowed to be a little bit sad that we missed out on some of the tiny moments or those firsts. It's finding the balance between wanting to be there for every moment and needing to have time for ourselves that is vital to our happiness and functioning.

I hope that by reading these three aspects of motherhood that have been challenging for me you are able to take a breath and realize that you are not the only mom out there who has experienced hardships in your parenting journey. My hardships may not be the exact same as yours, but I want you to remember that whether you openly talk about your struggles or not, I see you; I hear you; I know you; I am you. You're not alone in this wild rollercoaster ride of parenthood.

I'd love to hear from you about what resonated with you from this chapter. If you've been in the same boat, or even just the same ocean, please reach out! Momming is a wonderful job, but it's a damn hard one. There are no training manuals or annual workshops. So, let's stick together and build up our own toolboxes and resources.

You've got this, Mama!

CHAPTER 20

Carly Riding

FIND CARLY: **@CARLY_SUZ**

Nothing I have experienced in my life so far has sucked the life out of me more than having children. Sure, it fills my love tank (sometimes), but my sanity bank is running on empty most days. Baby brain is a thing, and I'm not sure if you ever fully get it back. I run on autopilot so much that I forget what I've just done, where I've put things, or how I've gotten here. The struggle is real — and it's been nine years.

If we knew exactly what was involved, would we still do it? No one told me it could be possible to have to deal with nighttime diapers with a seven-year-old, but here I am, and who knows for how much longer. If I'd have known, I would have bought stock in Pampers!

No one told me I would have to stay up until midnight so that the tooth fairy could come, making me a zombie at work the next day. Christmas Eve is a whole other story! And certainly no one told me that I would be a chef producing three different meals at dinner time since no kid likes the same foods, a housekeeper focusing on pee-covered toilets (aim for the Cheerios, boys) while vacuuming at the same time, a nighttime tutor for all the work they fall behind in at school because they are too busy being assholes in class, and a UFC referee of midget wrestling all in one evening. We never remember the bad parts — only the good ones — and I wouldn't have it any other way — but there are definitely hard days.

I grew up in England. My parents split when I was two years old. I didn't see my Dad very often so it was mainly me, my Mum, and my Gran, as I was an only child. I had no exposure to babies whatsoever, and I only had exposure to siblings through my friends, as my Mum was also an only child. I could never understand why my friends would fight with their siblings. I would have given anything to have one. So I always knew that I wanted to be a mum, and I always knew that I wanted two children. Not that it's bad being an only child, but I didn't want my child to be one. There are pros and cons to being an only child, but I always wanted them to have each other. I was in uncharted waters with sibling rivalry — that's for sure. It's a big thing between two boys. I'm sure every parent you talk to has a different idea of what the challenges of children are, but here are my momming hard challenges over the past nine years.

Birth plans often don't go to plan — or even make it out of your hospital bag (if you even have a hospital bag). A plan doesn't often go to plan; quite the oxymoron, isn't it? But it's true. My first pregnancy was textbook. I read *What to Expect When You're Expecting*. We went to prenatal classes, and watched 90s birth videos which scared the shit out of both of us (both the birth part and the 90s lack-of-personal-grooming part). I had a very detailed birth plan, including a list of items to bring to the hospital with us. When my first, Britt, was born, we didn't even have the car seat installed yet and the birth plan didn't even make it out of my purse, nevermind the non-existent hospital bag. I think we managed to grab a shopping bag with some pjs and a onesie for the baby. I didn't even have a chance to buy my post-birth giant granny panties yet. The main reason for this was that he was four weeks early, so you could say that we weren't quite prepared.

The carseat was still in the box and we had no hospital bag packed. Luckily the nursery was ready, but not the actual baby-coming-out-part ready. Not only did my perfect birth plan not happen, but the birth itself was also far from perfect. Labour was great. Well, as good as labour can be. I had an epidural and that made delivery like a workout for me. I was calm and controlled. But, he was corded pretty badly. He came out blue, and he was not breathing.

The first time I saw my son, he was being held upside down while a nurse slapped the soles of his feet trying to get him to breathe, but he was still struggling. Next thing I knew, he was taken to the NICU. One thing that did manage to happen on the birth plan is that Dad went with him. We always said if there were any issues with the baby, Dad must be there with him, and I will be just fine. So I lay there, with 2-3 people fiddling around down below. I couldn't feel a thing and I didn't know if my boy was going to make it or not. It was the worst 20 minutes of my life. I said to myself right then, if anything happens to this baby, they had better hide all roof access doors, 'cause I'm going skydiving without a parachute (it had been a rough couple of years, what can I say).

When his Dad returned with a photo of our boy all swollen, red and purple, tubes all over him, it was a tough moment. I've never felt so scared in my life, but he was going to be okay. We ended up in the NICU for six days. It was tough, but it was also great for me, being a new mum. It was like a new mummy boot camp and I was taught by the best, these incredible NICU nurses.

Babies are so delicate and I had never even changed a diaper before. I learned how to bathe, feed, burp, and swaddle (knowing how
to swaddle correctly is literally life changing for your first three
months together outside of your body). While learning these things
was helpful, it definitely wasn't how I expected my first week as a
mother to go, not even being at home.

Because Britt was oxygen deprived, I couldn't nurse him until they
had ruled out any digestive system tissue damage, which meant that
he had to be bottle fed. I was a milk machine for three days. When
he was ready to nurse, he was like hell no, what is this thing? This
is so much harder than a bottle. Give me my bottle! Breastfeeding
took like two weeks to master, and even then it wasn't pretty.
Breastfeeding is not unicorns and rainbows. I found it alienating
and painful having to leave the room to go pump for a solid 20
minutes. My FOMO would kick in, and sometimes I'd have to go
feed him just to relieve the pain and pressure. Poor kid was at a car
wash sometimes, getting nailed in the face by projectile milk before
I could latch him on. I just wasn't a fan and neither was Britt.

So the carseat was installed in the hospital parking lot, and we had
no clothes small enough to fit this tiny six-pound baby — so Dad
had to go buy some, along with some giant granny panties. Dad also
had to go home alone and leave us at the hospital, which I'm sure
was hard for him, too. We had no idea what to expect when we got
home, so we winged it and it went pretty well. So well, in fact, that
we decided to have another!

Baby number two had no birth plan since I knew they were shit
and I was already somewhat prepared. Talk about two completely
different births! You couldn't get more opposite. Finn came fast and
hard; there was no time for any medical intervention. As soon as
my water was broken he practically flew out, but since he was also
early — a whole five weeks early — I had to wait 20 minutes for the
paediatrician to arrive. If you'd have seen me during those 20 min-

utes you would have thought I was having an exorcism! I actually had a bulging membrane (if you aren't sure what that is, it's where the amniotic sac is actually bulging out of you).

Finn was a textbook birth. We did skin-to-skin instantly. He latched perfectly. That's probably why he's now a needy little bugger. I couldn't get this child off the boob and onto the bottle (probably partially my fault as it was so much easier with this baby). They couldn't have been more different. Aside from both being premature, they had completely different arrivals into the world.

Having two under two was a tornado, especially the first six months. So many moments like...What is happening here? Did I do this on purpose? Yes, yes you did, Carly. You aren't in control of anything whatsoever and you have to just relinquish whatever small amount of control you do have; there's nothing you can do about it. I didn't do too well with that.

For example, imagine driving home from a daycare pick up at the beginning of winter, so it's pitch black by 5 p.m. You arrive home and walk inside with your not-quite-two-year-old, and a one-month-old in a car seat. The not-quite-two-year-old with zero patience cannot wait long enough for you to put on the lights as you have a car seat in your hands, and runs head first into a dining room chair. There's a major meltdown in the dark, and now the baby joins in on the screaming fest. Meanwhile, your not-quite-two-year-old has a full on black eye and the next day is picture day.

Or picture giving your now-two-year-old a treat of KD for dinner (yes; that's a treat in our house) so that he will leave you alone while you nurse his little brother in the living room. He then proceeds to come sit on the couch with you with said KD, and spills it everywhere while eating, including on the dog. There is nothing you can do about it because your nipple is in a little person's mouth. OCD is kicking in big time at this point and you just have to let it happen.

My firstborn lured me into a false sense of security to have a second baby and wow, did I learn that no two children are alike — even two boys less than two years apart. Aside from his very traumatizing birth, Britt was a great baby. I had a regimented schedule. I wrote down everything, like everything, and I was even about to start sleep training him when he just decided to start doing it himself at around 8-weeks-old. Yes, we struggled with breastfeeding but he got the hang of it enough to do it when it was convenient, with bottles the rest of the time. It was a really great system. Just the two of us was pretty easy.

Now at nine years old, Britt is a handsome and stylish kid. You'll never see him without his hair done and a dapper outfit, but he has severe FOMO (fear of missing out). He is quite clearly the class clown and talks wayyyyyy too much. If there is a line to cross, Britt will cross it. He struggles with paying attention in school. He is naturally athletic and just an overall cool cat who we sometimes call "Britt the Brat" 'cause he can sure throw some attitude my way.

Finn, on the other hand, would not sleep through the night. He would not take a bottle and was totally attached to mummy. I still followed through with sleep training and bottle training because those things were important in our family and for our routine, but boy was it challenging. I even had to re-sleep train Finn at two years old as he had a sleep regression, which almost sent me to the looney bin. Finn didn't develop as fast as Britt either, which is unusual for a second-born. It's still that way to this day now he's seven. He's still very special in his own way. He is just a very unique little boy who beats to his own drum and who's favourite phrase is "God damn it" (insert slapping forehead emoji).

Finn is adorable in a cheeky way, but he has struggled in school from the beginning. Finn is just different — highly emotional and hot-headed. Finn actually pantsed a teacher at recess in Junior Kindergarten, at barely-four-years-old. I was simply mortified. With

Finn, we have been on the constant journey of IEP programs, a potential spectrum diagnosis (which has come up negative), and him constantly being behind in school.

But Finn is adorable beyond belief! The personality of this child is inspiring, and he is so smart. You should hear him talk about dinosaurs, fishing lures, or random facts like what the hottest pepper in the world is (it's the Carolina Reaper, if you were wondering, or at least it was back then). It's his emotional transitions and temper that hold Finn back and it can be really hard to manage, both at school and at home.

Yet, they are brothers, and they mean everything to each other. They do not like being apart at all and they make a pretty great beatboxing and rapping duo. They have different body types, personalities, emotional capabilities, interests, and abilities, yet they are hard to tell apart sometimes and can go from hating each other to best friends in the same minute. As soon as I think I've figured it out, they change something on me. I am the ringmaster of my own circus.

When the boys were five and three, their Dad and I separated. This was definitely a challenge, but it was the right decision. It was amicable and in the best interest of the boys — who were our main priority. I didn't want to stay together just for them. Coming from a single mom family myself, I knew they would be just fine. Some of you may disagree with me on this one and that's okay, but I think it's more important to show them a happy, healthy relationship for their own future standards of what a relationship should look like, rather than one that's not quite right. And I deserve to be happy too, don't I?

We aren't 50/50. We never were and we never will be based on jobs and our locations, and I'm ok with that. I knew going into the separation that they would be with me most of the time and their Dad every other weekend. I wouldn't change that, to be honest with you, even if he could have them more often. They have stability and a home base and get to go have fun with Dad on weekends and holidays, and it works for us.

I know that they miss their Dad and that part is tough for me to watch sometimes. It drives me insane that Dad is almost like a hero who swoops in every other weekend and gives them the time of their lives. There's not a single thought or moment of missing me because they are with me so much and they are having so much fun. Then they come back to me for the dreaded week of school. But that's okay, and I can bet that every other single mom out there feels the same way if they have a similar set up to me. I'm hoping that when my kids are older, they can see that mom can be fun too.

I'm not a single parent anymore. We are now a blended family. I have a step-daughter and my boys now have a sister who is with us 50/50. That brings a whole other bag of problems and a whole lot of awesomeness, too. But beware, blending is not for the faint-hearted. It can be harder than it would have been staying with their Dad, to be honest with you, but I love this man so incredibly much.

You have to remember that you are more than just a mom. You deserve to be happy, too! Being a mom completes me, but it certainly doesn't define me. I was Carly way before they came along, and you can't pour from an empty cup.

A single dad with a daughter, who has been a single dad since she was three, is a tough nut to crack. I still haven't cracked it, and I'm not sure if I ever will crack it. It is impenetrable and that's okay. We are truly quite blessed by how easily we blended, and we have been from day one. Everyone gets along (for the most part) and we all love each other, even though we aren't blood relatives. There will always be this division deep down between "them vs. us." I'm not sure if we will ever master being a "we" — and that's okay.

We didn't get a manual when we started this journey. We are basically making it up as we go along, as I'm sure families with both parents still together are, too. However, there will always be that "your kid" and "my kid" mentality which you just can't shake, and that brings a whole other dynamic of issues. It honestly is the only bone of contention between us — our children. He thinks my boys get away with everything, and I think his daughter gets away with everything. How do you come to a common ground there? You don't. You just learn to live with a slight divide and get on with it. They're all ten and under right now, and I can't even begin to imagine the issues we will have with teenagers, but underneath it all, at the core, we are a good fit and there's a lot of love there. No matter what, we will figure it out.

Nine times out of ten whenever we fight or have words, children are the subject. That's a tough pill to swallow sometimes. They are who they are, and for the most part, we actually *disagree* on what we consider to be acceptable and unacceptable. I think this is because I have been with my boys a lot — and two boys 80% of the time is a lot more than one girl 50% of the time. So while I have had to learn to pick my battles and not sweat the small stuff, he hasn't had to do that. He has babied his daughter because he misses her so much when she isn't home. She has been his only everything for a long time, which is okay, but she doesn't get her own set of rules because he only sees her half of the time. He also sees my two boys more than he sees his own child, and I feel that there is a little resentment toward us for that. Not that he can help it, and I can totally understand where that comes from, but sometimes it's unfair — and it isn't our fault. Can you see? It's tough, but it's been over three years now and we are a family with a lot of love there.

Now I'm 40 and when I look back on the last ten years, it's a blur. Some parts don't even seem real. So much has happened. So much has changed; some for the better, some for the worse. It has been really challenging. I've felt totally alone. My children and my relationships have sent me to the edge and back. I've had to sacrifice my career to have more work-life balance. I've lost my sense of self from time to time. We've had to move as we outgrow our space. I have 20 lb of every love humps that I do not care for, and I'm pretty sure I'm going to need a part-time job just to feed these guys as they get older. It's been tough — really tough.

When I look at the next ten years, I'm excited to see them grow and become young adults. I want to go on adventures with them and show them the world. They are going to be much better young men because they now have a sister in their lives, and I hope that they treat every relationship they ever have with the same admiration that they have for her. And boy, do they love their momma. I cannot describe the feeling of looking into your child's eyes to see yourself looking back at you. Momming is definitely HARD, but nothing worthwhile is ever easy.

CHAPTER 21

Brooke Shaughnessey

FIND BROOKE: **@BROOKESHAG**

Motherhood: Creating My Own Box

Trigger Warning — Suicide

I am a mother of three amazing children. Cora (CL), Sophie (Sis) and Harley (Har). I am that mom who is an overachiever and "perfect" due to anxiety. I live in Lakefield, Ontario, and I have loved to write since I was a young child. If I am not writing then I am singing with my children — anything from Fleetwood Mac to Billie Eilish. I am the youngest of three and I grew up in a hilarious household that was filled with love and inappropriate jokes. My mom raised us while our dad was on the road, and she is someone I have learned everything from. I give her credit for me being a strong, independent woman. Currently I am in school to be a PSW, and will hopefully bridge to nursing. Everything I do in my life I do for my children. I have many goals, and writing has always been one of them. I love to sit and watch the kids skateboard or play in the grass while I write things that make no sense at the time. Life is too short to not do what we love.

When we have our children we want to be that "perfect" mom; the person we see in the magazine who is doing everything we think we have to do, too. There is pressure to hand make all the baby eats and wears, to use reusable diapers, and to only breastfeed.

I was terrified to be a mom at 24. I was overweight, struggled from anxiety, and sucked at cleaning. I loved to cook but it seemed like so much pressure. Imagine the day I took Cora to the doctor for her six-week check-up. She wasn't getting enough breastmilk and I was asked to switch to formula. I felt like a failure and called my mom right away. *Why can't I breastfeed like everyone else? Am I a bad mom? Will she grow as well as other children if she's on formula?* Sadly, I knew nothing about formula. I listened to everyone else and read everything to be that 'perfect' mom. Thankfully, it didn't take long for her to gain weight. I felt so silly trying to fit into a box. Never in my life have I fit into a box, so why did I think that being a mom would be different? This is when my parenting style changed. This is when I started to listen to my gut instincts and stay calm in emergencies — both big and small.

I have always joked to friends and family that I'm a single mom, even when I was married to my husband. He was always on the road working on pipelines, and I was home raising our three children. I was that person who was there planning all of the holidays and family functions. I rarely ever had another person help take over bath time, dinner time, or even to bring the kids to soccer, lacrosse, gymnastics, or skating. Due to these moments in my life, I truly started to feel like I was a single mom, but with the support of income coming in from another person.

Most people ask me how I am not "crazy" and how I do it alone all the time. With my husband on the road and my three kids busy in sports, you would probably see me as insane, too. I did this on purpose though. I would stay busy all day long so I wouldn't have to think about my own problems. I only had to focus on my children and what makes them happy, never focusing on what I wanted, and, more importantly, needed. I would make sure that everyone was early for their sport, and I would always be their cheerleader. I was there to help them gear up and I was there to tell them "We will get 'em next time!!!" As mothers we forget to think of ourselves, and then we tend to live in survival mode because it helps us to get from Point A, a pee break at Point C, and running all the way to Point Z.

I am that mom who picks and chooses her battles. You might get upset with your children for being loud in the other room or fighting with each other, but what I hear is happiness and them finally interacting with each other. You might run to your child when they yell, "Mom, Tommy kicked me!!!!" I would say "Are ya bleeding?" You might get worried if your kids are outside too long. I am just excited that my kids are getting fresh air and using their imaginations — we can eat our dinner later today. I had to adjust my mindset very early in this motherhood adventure, or I wouldn't have survived it. Mothering is so hard. When we put too much thought into being perfect and it doesn't happen — this is when we become anxious, sad, mad, jealous, and really any mucky emotion you can think of. Shifting your focus on things you can control is when you gain your control back. You can finally feel free, and maybe laugh at stuff you would have gasped at before.

My daughters, Cora and Sophie, were born fourteen months apart. From day one they would tell everyone that they were twins, and would never leave each other's side. When one was being breastfed, the other was being bottle fed in the other arm. I'm lucky that I am strong, because I was constantly carrying two babies around. Everything I did for one, the other had to have or do as well. When one was sleeping, the other was awake. I swear they planned it and were trying to see if I would survive. Would I crack under the constant stress and lack of sleep? No way! Can't get rid of me that easily. I ate little, lived on coffee, and fell asleep when I was able to. I will not generalize, but it's funny that some men don't even bat an eye when a baby cries. We get up while being half asleep, change that bum while half asleep, feed the baby while half asleep, and wonder if we dreamt that or did Sally sleep through the night last night? Don't worry though, Bob had a great sleep!

Sophie is the child who you worry about. She has zero fear, and for a mom that is usually alone, that's scary. She is now 10, but when she was younger she loved Tinkerbell. She once thought, "Well if Tink can fly, so can I!!!!" I was nine months pregnant with my son and I walked in to find her jumping off a tall bed, the largest smile on her perfect little face, and boom, blood! Instead of panicking, I got surgical tape and taped the gaping hole under her mouth closed. I was nine months pregnant with Harley, had Cora and Sophie, and alone with no babysitter. I sadly did what I could do at the time; I taped her up and prayed that it would heal. I acted quickly without panic and she didn't even notice.

Three years before this incident I broke a candle. As I left the room for one minute to grab the broom, Sophie was somehow able to run, jump on the glass, and cut her foot very badly. I grabbed elastics as a makeshift tourniquet and rushed to the hospital. She lost too much skin to stitch it all back up, so she was injected with freezing until the blood stopped. This is not even close to an exhaustive list of her mishaps, nor will it be the last hospital trip for Sophie. We can talk about her skateboarding and breaking her growth plate. Or her running at school and her head crashing into a fence. Luckily my husband was able to rush her to the hospital in a calm manner. There was no crying, just stitches and popsicles. You get the picture here; I had to focus on not panicking and staying calm for my children. When we are anything but calm in moments like these, it makes it so much harder for them. We pull out those masks all mothers have.

How many masks do you have? Probably too many to count, like me. I find that my friends can't stand my "coffee ordering mask." It's slightly fake and always happy. They always ask, "Why do you do that?" Well, think of it this way: if that person is having a crappy day and everyone has treated them like a piece of trash, they feel worthless and just need to see a bright smile. I will always be that person. I will always give my light to make others feel even just a little bit happier if I can. In my neighborhood I am called mom by over 20 children. They even knock on my door just to hug me. The mask I use and alway have on for them is my "mask of compassion." I am always that empathic ear for them. I am always that mom who will have food for all the other kids in the area. I will always be that person who will give you a hug if you need it, because hugs are healing and kids need hugs and extra love.

Masks don't have to be a bad thing. We all have masks for all different situations in life. When my husband's best friend killed himself in 2018, I had to have that "mask of strength." I wanted to break down more than I did, but I pushed through for the kids. I cried alone a lot. They knew exactly how he died, and it was horrifying to me that they knew. A six-year-old and a seven-year-old knew how their uncle died, and now I have to explain mental health and suicide to them. We talked about drugs and why Uncle D felt the way that he did. We talked about Daddy and we promised we would help if and when he needed it. Those conversations required double masking — the "mask of education" and the "mask of strength."

Cora decided to sing a song for her uncle at the school talent show. She sang "One More Light" by Linkin Park, and there wasn't a dry eye in that auditorium, except for me. I hid my "sensitive mask" that night at the talent show. I knew that if I was a mess and cried, she would be embarrassed and think that I didn't like her performance. I had a smile on my face the entire time while my best friend cried so hard beside me. I had that choking sensation in my throat — the feeling when you are fighting off those tears — just trying so hard to rock that smile for my beautiful star up on the stage. I cried in the shower that night when I got home. I was so proud of her and the song choice was well beyond her years.

Sometimes in life we need to put on the mask that I call "Braveheart." It's a "William, I am your uncle" kind of mask. Sophie was struggling with school and I needed to fight for her. I needed to be her voice. "Braveheart" came out to play. I didn't quit. I fought hard for her until years later when she finally got an IEP, a social worker, and into the empowerment program designed by SickKids hospital.

Masks also help me when I am struggling with my anxiety. It helps me hide it and continue to function in daily life. Anxiety comes in so many forms. Mine makes me overtalk, hold my breath, experience chest pain, overthink everything I do in life, and it also makes me overachieve. I have struggled with self-doubt my entire life, always thinking I was never good enough, but you would never know this unless we are super close.

Most people think that I have it easy. I am always laughing. I have all the time in the world to volunteer. I am the best mom and my kids are so great. Well, first off, I cry more than anyone will ever know. My anxiety is what makes me overachieve and sign up for 100 events. My kids are hilarious, yes, but they fight 24/7 and sometimes they are mean to me. I have no time to go to the washroom or eat in a day, but somehow I make everything else work out.

It took the separation from my husband for me to realize that I need to take time for myself. I need to focus on my anxiety, and maybe slow down for the kids. It's okay to overachieve; it's okay to volunteer; it's okay to always be laughing and showing that you are happy. But ask yourself: are you being the true you, or are you only wearing those masks? If I could give you any advice, it would be to *breathe*. Those kids over there, looking at you, think you are the best thing on Earth!

My children are hilarious. They are well beyond their years when it comes to jokes and life in general. No matter where I am or what I am doing, I instantly laugh when I think about them. They tell me random facts while I am drinking coffee, like "Mom, when you die, they put a butt plug in you. Gotta plug it up," and I respond with "Please don't search that on Google images!!!!!"

They are the reason that I am still alive, and why I am the way I am today. They are constantly dancing, singing, and laughing. Don't let this fool you, they also do their fair share of fighting, screaming, and crying. We never know if someone is going to leave slime on the couch or if someone is going to throw a ball through the window. It's just a rollercoaster full of laughs, screams, and asking *I wonder what's next?*

Being a mom is hard — really freaking hard. It's a never-ending job that can make you cry, fall apart, or make you feel drained and exhausted. But remember, it's also very rewarding — and it's something that naturally comes to us. We mould to our situations. We don't let our children see our hurt, our breakdowns, or our heartbreaks. We mostly show them our shining sides.

My son, Harley, wakes up and always gives me the biggest hug in the world with a kiss. He tells me that I am his favourite girl in the city (city is the world to him). He has the gentlest soul with the strength of a farmer. He and his sisters like to challenge me daily and keep me on my toes.

When I was in my early 20s and late teens, I wished I was dead. I felt like this world didn't need me in it. I now think back and think of how silly that sounds. I am very important to three beautiful children. I never thought anyone could love someone like me.

Three kids later, I have learned so much. I am worthy of love, laughs, and hugs. I can wake up with a smile knowing that, an hour later, I will be kissed and hugged by three grumpy trolls. I wake up every day knowing that my body created these incredible souls. I work harder every day because of them. I went back to school recently so I can show them what a strong, independent, single woman looks like. It's time to shine even brighter than before. What mask will be in my hobo purse today? Who knows, but it will be one that can be mouldable to my situation. Do you need a hug, a shoulder to cry on, or someone just to talk to? No matter your age, I will be there. Do you need advice or a stern talking to? I have those masks in there, too, don't worry. I will always be there for anyone who needs me, especially my children, and I make sure that they know that. I openly talk about my anxiety, and they know when I am having low days. Those days look like coffee and chocolate, but I always come out on top.

My hope for my children is that they are the change that this world needs. They are those souls that will help anyone in need, and that when they get older, they can be the mom or dad energy to 20 children in their neighborhood. I have hopes that they make all of the people they meet in life feel safe and secure. I hope that they don't struggle with anxiety or their mind in general like I do, and that they learn to love who they are now before they feel forced to carry several masks with them. I hope that their father and I have taught them to love so that they have healthy relationships with friends and partners. They might always roll their eyes at me for the things that I do, but one day they will do these same things and say with a laugh, "I look just like my mom right now!" They will hopefully realize then that all of those crazy things I have done that make me look like I am the "perfect" mom will help them for the future.

What I have learned on this journey is that it's okay to create our own box. Heck, mine is made up of rose quartz, amethyst, a sex joke, and coffee. My best friends' boxes are made of wine, dad jokes, and chocolate — and we are all still friends. We don't have to be in the same box to love each other, be a part of each other's village, build each other up, and help raise each other's children. We have zero judgement for how we parent, and we laugh at the same things.

I wish that I realized when I was becoming a mother that I didn't have to fit into a certain box, but here we are today. I'm here telling you to shine! Be that beautiful hexagon if that is what you choose to be. Add some colour, some eggplant stickers, and maybe even some sparkle. Whatever you're doing, you're doing it right. Keep doing you, you magical unicorn. Create your own box.

CHAPTER 22

Lisa Southall

FIND LISA: **@ILLUMINATEYOURSOUL_LSOUTHALL**

I write this chapter being on the other side of Momming Hard. I've made it to the side of momming that's *after* the phase when your children need you and rely on you for their wellbeing. I am here to tell you that yes, you can do it, even though there will be many times when you fear that you cannot.

I am 53 years old and the proud mom of three beautiful adult daughters. I will share my story of the struggles that I had in my 17-year abusive marriage, which led to divorce and single momming for 13 years, all while battling PTSD and mental health challenges from the abuse. I will share with you that it was hard — emotionally, physically, and financially — however, it was also some of my most beautiful and cherished times in my life, witnessing my young daughters flourish into adults and being happy and successful in their own lives.

Maybe some parts of this are resonating with you, or maybe all of it is. This is why I have chosen to be vulnerable and share my story of raising children through the difficult times. These are times when you may feel lonely, exhausted, and like there is no end to the "raising" of children with little or no support from the other parent. Or possibly, like my experience, there was no support from the other parent — only chaos.

My hopes and intentions in writing this chapter are to share with you the coping mechanisms that I used when my mental health was at its lowest and most difficult point. I will discuss the coping mechanisms that I learned from people who I know that I was "universally aligned" with, as well as those who I sought professional help from. I knew that I had to feel better for my daughters' sake, because I wanted to be the best and most present mom that I could be under the circumstances.

I am proud, relieved, and happy to say that I am healed from the trauma of abuse, and that my PTSD and mental health are definitely better and manageable. During this journey of healing, discovery, and divulging my trauma, I found my life's purpose.

They say that your pain is your purpose. I, therefore, now understand that the pain that I went through during my marriage, divorce, and single parenting was meant to be shared. During the past five years I have developed and am a certified Energy Healing Intuitive, working with Universal energy and using Reiki and Crystals to heal the energy one holds in their body from trauma.

This is my journey that I share with you — to give light and hope during those hard times that you may feel that you cannot cope with momming during the difficult times.

We met at a young age, at a church Youth Group. I was 15 and Eric was 18, my first boyfriend. This is important to know, as he was my first and only boyfriend, whom I then married. I did not know what a relationship was supposed to be like and how I was to be treated, or how to communicate in a relationship. There were warning signs in the beginning. He would get angry easily with me, and we would fight often. I know in the beginning we were in love with each other. We had common interests and the sense of family was important to both of us.

I was raised to believe that a girl grew into a woman, found a man, got married, had children, and raised a family. All of my role models growing up solidified this path. I understood that relationships were not always meant to be good, and that there were rough times along with the good times, so I did not really question whether our relationship was healthy or not.

After eight years of dating, we were married. We had our challenges in our marriage, but there was one thing that we did agree on, and that was that we wanted to have children. We wanted to become a family.

Four years into our marriage our first daughter, Maddison, was born. I will never forget that feeling of becoming a mom, holding my baby for the first time. I thought that my heart was going to burst. I knew that I was responsible for this "little human," and that every decision and action I made would impact her. I remember on the day we left the hospital thinking, *what now? What do I do with this little human? I have no clue what I am doing.* I joked with Eric to not forget to pack the instruction manual. I was joking; however, I was also being serious. If only children came with an instruction manual. There is so much unknown, and no two children are alike.

I was working and was on maternity leave, which at that time was only six months long. I absolutely loved being a mom. In fact, when

I was younger and people would ask me what I wanted to be when I grew up, my answer was always "to be a mom."

The first couple of months were absolutely challenging. Settling into new routines, figuring out how to be a mom, making sure that I was doing all the right things. However, all in all, momming was something that I felt natural at and loved.

When my maternity leave was over, I was not ready to leave Maddison with a caregiver. I wanted to be there for her and not a stranger. I shared my feelings with Eric. I wasn't ready and I wanted to stay home with Maddison, but he would not agree with me and said that we needed my income to be able to keep our house and raise a family. I did go back to work and left Maddison with a caregiver, but it was only for a short while, as I was so distraught and begged Eric to please let me stay home and raise our daughter. He did agree, as long as we made changes to our lifestyle. I was so thankful that I could be a stay-at-home mom.

Two years later our second daughter Karleigh was born. I did not think that my heart could love any more than it already did; however, the minute I laid eyes on Karleigh my heart grew even bigger. Maddison and Karleigh were only 22 months apart, and watching Maddison love her little sister and wanting to be a part of taking care of her was magical to witness.

I loved being an at-home mom. We had settled into many routines and children groups like gymnastics, library groups, and children's play groups. I was very close with my family, especially with my mom, and we saw each other almost every day.

When the girls were three and one, we moved away due to Eric's work. We moved over 500 kilometers away from our families. This was a huge adjustment, and was the beginning of our really tough times as a married couple. I was extremely unhappy being so far away from my family, and to make things worse, his new job had him travelling — a lot and often — usually a couple of weeks at a time.

So here I was new to the city, alone with no family or support, raising two young children. It was the beginning of my depression, the feeling of hopelessness, loneliness, and the feeling of my voice not being heard. I would share with Eric how I was really missing my family, and would he please consider moving back to our hometown where each of our families were so that I would have support when he travelled. He would always say, "No; this is where my job is, and if you want a roof over your head, this is where we will have to live. You will just have to learn to live with it."

I didn't realize it at the time, and I never really questioned the behaviour or actions of Eric, but his actions were full of control, manipulation, fear, guilt, and obligation. The term that is often heard now is "gaslighting." Moving me away from my family and my support was part of the controlling behavior, creating isolation. We would often fight over money, that I spent too much and that we didn't have enough. The fights never ended with a resolution, just further walls between us. There was what he thought and felt, and what I thought and felt. We were growing apart due to a lack of communication or understanding one another's thoughts, opinions, or cares.

To those people that were around us — friends we had made in the new city, neighbours, and even our own families — we looked and seemed like we were a happy family. I had gotten really good at pretending that I was okay. This was a façade that I would put on that helped me cope. It was important to me that the girls' happiness and wellbeing was the priority. I would focus on the joy that being a mom brought to me to help me through those tough days. I was happy being a mom and caring for our children. Mom was my identity; it was who I was and who I was most happy being — a loving and caring mom.

Even though we were struggling as a couple we decided to have a third child. I know you are thinking, *what the hell? Another child will not solve your marital problems.*

Maddison was five and Karleigh was three when Zoey joined our family. She was a ray of sunshine in our family unit. I was fully immersed in raising three children under the age of five and loving every minute of it. I loved the neighbourhood play dates and lunches with other at-home moms. It was a world I absolutely loved.

Seventeen years into our marriage, I could no longer take being married. Our marriage fell apart for many reasons. Before separating, I did seek out the help from a therapist for the way that I was feeling. I expressed that I was depressed being away from my family, and how I found communicating and living with Eric so difficult and emotionally exhausting. It was during the process of therapy that it brought to my attention that I was in an emotionally abusive marriage. Eric and I sought out couples' therapy in hopes that maybe having someone mediate us and our arguments would help bring resolution to our issues. Unfortunately, this was not the case, and we decided to separate.

For one year we continued to live in the same house so that the children would not be affected with their schooling and have to transition from one house to another. After four months of the five of us living together, we decided that the tension and stress was too much. We decided that one of the parents would live in the house one week with the girls, and then live one week out of the house, keeping the girls living at the house the entire time for stability.

Our matrimonial home finally sold after a year-and-a-half. Custody and divorce proceedings could finally commence. Why would I ever think that a divorce would go smoothly when in our marriage we could not communicate and figure things out amicably? It was an ugly and gruesome divorce, which involved mediators, lawyers, and a child psychologist. In the end we finally agreed on custody and a shared parenting agreement; however, our communication with each other and transitions between homes were ugly. It usually involved us fighting or the girls crying because they didn't want to leave the other parent.

The immense stress of the divorce was taking its toll on my mental health. I sought medical help for depression and anxiety that I was experiencing, and was at that time diagnosed with PTSD due to the trauma of the many years of emotional abuse. In addition, because custody and divorce proceedings took so long, I was financially struggling and was working one full-time job and two part-time jobs to keep the roof over the heads of the girls and myself.

Two years into our separation and having a custody schedule of week on and week off, Eric decided on one of his weeks with the girls to drop the girls off back at my house, and told the girls to live with me. From that day on, I have been single parenting the girls. From that day on, the girls' father was barely in their lives, and in the past four years, pretty much not at all.

The girls were heading into their pre-teen and teen years — the hormonal years — where influences of friends and society can affect children's behaviour. I was working approximately 60-70 hours a week and running a home and a household of three kids — ensuring schoolwork was being completed, being an emotional support for those tough days at school socially and academically, after school activities, friend dates, keeping the house clean, grocery shopping, cooking meals — the list goes on for the demands that were on me as a single parent. I was losing my mind, and my patience was very thin. I was exhausted all the time, every day!

All of this was going on while also reeling in mental health complications. I was burning out. I was stressed financially. I was burning the candle at both ends working and running a home. There was absolutely no "me time." One day I had a complete meltdown and knew that I could not go on continuing the way that I was.

My therapist recommended that I seek the help of a Neural Structural Chiropractor named Tony, and a Life Coach named Kae, who were gathering data for a program they were developing to cure PTSD. This was the first step in my true healing from all of the trauma of my marriage. It was also my first introduction into energy healing and meditation. Energy healing intrigued me. I could feel the healing benefits of understanding how trauma is captured in the body. It affects your emotions and your behaviours.

I decided to become certified in Reiki so that I could help other people heal from their trauma too. I read many books on understanding energy and healing from energy. Healing the energy in my body was the key to recovering from PTSD, depression, and anxiety. Depression stems from living in the past, dwelling on it, rethinking it, and punishing yourself for past actions. Anxiety comes from worrying about the future, what will happen if...? Learning to live in the now and not have the negative energy in our bodies creates peace and healing.

I was so thankful to find this new way of living peacefully with mindfulness, nature walks, being in the now, meditation, yoga, and giving and receiving as much Energy Healing as I could. All of this was bringing peace and balance back into my life so that I could once again enjoy being a mom. Even if it was still stressful and chaotic at times managing my work and life balance, I knew I had a coping mechanism to rebalance myself.

I was able to enjoy all of the girls' milestones like getting their first jobs, winning soccer or rugby matches, successes in school grades, school plays, graduating from high school, college, and university. There is a feeling of pure joy and so much pride when your child walks across that graduation stage. I also watched with pride as they became engaged to be married, moved out on their own, and developed their careers. Their life skills allowed them to become strong, independent, and hard working women in society.

I have especially enjoyed their young adult lives. The bonds that we have created over the years as a unit — our family of four is impenetrable. I am most proud of the family unit that we have become.

In the beginning, I struggled with not being a "typical" family; Mom, Dad, and children. I have peacefully come to realize that "family" can come in any formation. Our formation of mom and three daughters is our family, and we support, love, uplift, and encourage each other daily. Don't get me wrong, a household full of women can be filled with a lot of emotion and opinions, but at the end of the day, we love each other so deeply and would do anything for one another.

I want you to know that momming is tricky, and it's sticky. Sometimes we feel like we are drowning. How can I manage this full schedule of "to-do's" today? How can I pay the bills? How can I buy groceries? Am I making all the right decisions when raising the girls? These are decisions that I was making alone since their father was not in their lives. Should they hang out with that person? Are they trying hard enough in school? Am I parenting them enough because I am spreading myself thin between work and momming? Have I been compassionate enough in a situation? All of these are questions that I most likely answered "no" to most of the time. That's okay. At least I showed up and I was in their lives. What I mean is...don't be so hard on yourself. You are doing the best that you can do each and every day. Raising decent humans is a really hard job, but what we have to remember as humans ourselves is that we can only do what we are capable of. As long as you are trying your hardest and showing up each and every day, you're doing wonderfully.

Here are my tips: Keep yourself healthy. Make sure you eat right, and exercise or at least move your body every day. Get outside in all types of weather and enjoy nature. Find things that bring you joy. Don't punish yourself because of those not-so-great decisions that you made — or if you were too tired to get something done. Make sure that you take time for yourself. Meditate if you can, and center yourself. Don't dwell in the past or worry about the future. Reach out to a friend or fellow mom who is good at listening and can be compassionate. Get your frustrations off of your chest, and get the energy out of your body. Be present for your kids; that's all they need.

CHAPTER 23

Melissa Stentiford

FIND MELISSA: **@LIFEWITHMISSA**

Hello! My name is Melissa and I am a proud mama of two (ages 17 and 4). I have the most incredible man beside me every day. We live in Georgina, Ontario, and I hail from Bobcaygeon, Ontario. Yes; the little town with the world's best ice cream and that the amazing Tragically Hip sings about. I speak two languages. My first is sarcasm (yes; it is a language), and English is my second language. My mind lives in the gutter, and I have a habit of making almost all statements dirty. ;) By day I split my time between being a woman, a mom, a wife, a school bus driver, and a health, wellness, and mindset coach. I truly love helping people — especially women — find their inner sass and love for themselves! Follow along with us on Instagram *@lifewithmissa.*

Okay, so now that we've gotten to know each other a bit, I want you to lean in real close, 'cuz I'm going to let you in on a little secret. Are you ready? Listen carefully...PENIS!!! Kidding...I just wanted to make sure that I have your attention. Alright, joking aside, here is the *actual* big secret:

Being a mom is not hard.

Now wait, wait, Wait, WAIT!...Don't throw the book; don't close the book; and don't turn my pages. Don't call me that! That was quite unladylike. Just give me a minute to explain.

If you look up the definition of "mom" in the dictionary, you will see "a female parent." That seems like a simple, very clear definition, right? However, being a mom is not that simple — and we all know that.

You know what makes being a mom hard? It's being the mom that everyone expects you to be. We are all trying to compete and be the mom that society and the other moms in our lives tell us to be. When we become a mom we get an overload of advice (yes; most comes from love). From other moms, to complete strangers, to other females in our life — they all feel that they know what's best. Sometimes the advice from other moms is helpful, but then there are times that the advice comes across as criticism (and not in the constructive way, either).

Look back in history. When did the shift happen? When did being a mom mean being able to put on the most amazing birthday party? Or competing for the best gluten-free dessert? And then there's the pressure to look a certain way, too, which should have absolutely *NOTHING* to do with being a mom. But here we are, looking at each other and competing...and if you think about it, we are making this competition harder and harder every day. We keep hearing and saying, "Raising kids today is very different than it was years ago." — and it very much is. But what if we shifted some of our thoughts and actions? Maybe we could make it easier on ourselves, and make it a little easier on future moms. I am no professional and have only been a mom for 17 years, but I'm going to tell you what I've learned — and how I'm shifting my thoughts and actions to make being a mom easier for me.

I joined the mom club at 22. I didn't even know who I was, so I didn't have the confidence or the self-esteem to be the mom that I felt I should be. Looking back, I can see that I did not love myself enough to love another adult, let alone this child that was growing inside of me. Then, to add salt to the wound as they say, shortly after her first birthday my eldest's father decided that he wanted his life back, and that we were taking up too much of his time.

I wish I could say that between the time I was a first-time mom to the time I had my second daughter that I had learned and fixed my mistakes, but alas, I cannot. For 16 years I did what most do. I was trying to be the mom that others have told me I should be. I listened to the advice and the instructions given by others. I knew growing up — something we have probably all said many times — that I didn't want to parent the way that we were parented. But because of my lack of confidence and not knowing myself well enough, I was falling back on how I was raised. There was also the fact that she and I were living with my parents. And because they had helped with raising her, there was guilt every time that I wanted to speak up or do things differently, so I didn't. I would let them parent or do what I thought *they* would do. I was not open to the fact that my child was not me. She was and is very different from me, and I have come to learn that that is an extremely important fact when raising these little humans.

I was raised to believe that if you made a mistake, forgot something, or anything that they felt was "wrong," you got yelled at for it. Well, in all honesty, that means that I was yelled at a lot...because I seem to make mistakes and forget things a lot. Instead of breaking that cycle,

I let those outside voices dictate that that's how you're supposed to raise a child. My child needed explanations and reasons…not yelling. She is a person that does not handle anger and confrontation very well, and she internalises her emotions. In fact, she gets sick because of this. But I did not know this and I did not pay attention to this. I would tell her to "grow up" or "stop being a baby." And because of that, I actually ended up failing as a mother and as a parent.

One of my biggest regrets is that for those years, I did not raise my eldest the way that she should have been raised. I did not love her the way that she needed to be loved. This was brought to my attention by her in a not-so-gentle way. One night after dinner, she made a joking remark about me giving her a hug, but then it quickly changed into a serious conversation and she told me that she was sad and mad that I didn't love her the way I love her sister. She's told me that she feels that I don't love her enough. I am not proud of that, and to say that her comment wasn't a kick in the gut and a punch in the heart would be a lie. I have never had any comment in my life hit me the way that that one did. It hit hard because of how true it was.

On the flip side, though, I am incredibly proud of her and I feel blessed that she felt safe enough to tell me how she was feeling. I wish I could say that after she told me that I had a brilliant response and apology for her, but I did not. Instead, I hid within myself and really let it soak in. Her comment made me truly look back and realize that she was right.

I am not saying that I love one daughter more than the other, but I certainly did *show* the love differently. With the eldest, I was young and did not want to be a mom. I felt very alone during my pregnancy, and did not "enjoy" it at all. When she was born, I did not feel that click with her right away. She was such a good baby, too. The pregnancy was easy (just believe me when I say that, because if I explain fully, you'll get mad at me again), and from her first night, seriously, night one, she has slept through the night. (I'm talking six to seven straight hours for the first couple of weeks, then the full eight hours). She was a happy and smart little one, too, but there was always this missing piece for me.

I don't really know when it all clicked, but at some point I realized that the missing piece was me — and not her. I was holding onto past resentment and lack of parental love, and I was raising her the same way. I wasn't listening to her or really *seeing* her for who she was — and who she was growing into. I was not being fair to her at all. It was me that I didn't love, not her!! Then, when her father left, instead of holding her tighter I pushed her away. Again, the anger came back, and I was jealous that he got to "have a life" and I was "stuck with her."

Of course this all comes back to me and my inner battles; this was not her fault at all. Once I opened my heart and my mind to these realizations, I was able to start working on being a better version of myself.

I am still a work in progress with my parenting choices, and that was made clear to me when my youngest heart-punched me with her own comment. That's when I really decided to shift myself. At the tender age of three, she looked at me one day after she had spilled her dry cereal on the floor and said "you're not yelling." I took a minute and looked at her and said "What do you mean?" She looked at me with big brown eyes and said "You're not mad I spilled?" and I said "No; you didn't mean to do it." And in that moment while hugging her to apologize, I realized that's how she looks at me. My three-year-old is looking at me as the mom who yells.

The shift has not been easy. It was hard to fight off that voice inside of me that was telling me how to be the right mom for my girls. It's just as hard, if not harder, to block out the outside voices that are telling me that what I'm doing is wrong, but it's the voice inside — that gut feeling, that intuition — that is the voice that we need to listen to. Once I started listening to that voice, it caused strain in relationships in my life, and it caused people to lash out and be very angry and resentful toward me. I know now, however, that in order to be a better mom, a stronger mom, and a more loving mom, that I *need* and *have* to follow that inner voice.

I'm beginning to realize that these pages that you're reading — this is my apology to my eldest. This is my explanation to her. It is not an excuse, and it is not going to make up for the way that I failed her, but I am hoping that she will read these pages and see that I didn't do it purposefully. I was just being the mom that I thought I had to be, not the mom that I *should* be. I have so much love for her. The person I was having trouble loving was — and is — me.

Another big obstacle that I have had to overcome, when being a mom and in life, is that I am a selfish person. I say that meaning that I think of myself first (yes; even before my kids and my man). I have been a selfish person my whole life. I only ever wanted to do what made me happy, eat what made me feel good, or go where I wanted to go. As a kid, when I didn't get my way I went quiet and got very scornful. As an adult, when I'm told *No*, it's still the same. A prime example of this is when I found out that I was pregnant with my first. I was *ANGRY*. Then when somebody would tell me that being a mom is about putting your child first, I found it very difficult to accept that. It's not that I wouldn't accept the words. It's that I can't wrap my mind around them. I don't know how to process that statement and actually follow through with it.

So part of my journey as a mom, and a woman, has been learning that I am allowed to be me! I am a more present person for those around me when I take care of myself first, when I accept that part of me, and when I start to love that part of me. Over the last 18 months I have made it my goal to show up for me. I have been showing my girls that I matter, and that I'm just as important, if not more important, than them. If I'm not healthy and happy, how can I make sure that they are? And what kind of example am I setting for them when I always put myself second, third, or fourth behind them and their dad? I want my girls to continue to break this mom's cycle, and they have to see me do it in order for them to learn it.

It has not been easy. In fact, this is the hardest journey that I've ever been on. I am constantly told what a bad, selfish, and ignorant mother I am. I get questioned every day on my personal or parenting choices. I am told that my wants and needs should be coming after those of my children, but it's not like I'm taking food from them or using money to buy myself things and leaving them with no clothes. I am simply taking *time* for me. And again, I don't usually do this during the times they need me. I get up before they even think of being awake. I stay up after they've gone to bed. I heard somebody once say that a bad mom is the one that doesn't feel guilty, not the ones that do.

Well, then, I guess at times I'm a bad mom — and honestly, I'm good with that. You see, when I sit down to read my book, write in my journal, work out in the morning, or try to sit and write these pages while my girls are doing something else, I don't feel guilty that I'm not spending time with them. I look at it as showing them independence. They also need to see that we need to love ourselves before we can truly love another — even our children.

This is what I want for my girls. I want them to grow up strong, smart, and self-reliant. I need to know that they will have — and use — their own voices. I need them to see that they are important and that they matter. They need to know that they are responsible for their own happiness. Others will come into their lives to add to it, but at the end of the day, being happy is their choice! I always want them to feel safe and loved, but also be able to feel and express their feelings and thoughts! They need to *LOVE* themselves. I am shocked to say that I feel the most proud of my girls when they speak up to me or others. It's important that they speak and show their feelings and their opinions.

Sometimes, when they've expressed themselves, I've made the mistake of taking it personally or as disrespect, but in reality, it is them just doing and showing me (or whoever they're speaking to) who they are and what they want. We should be applauding them for this, not disciplining for "lack of respect." I am not saying that a child should be yelling at their parents when they're told no for things, but I am saying that we, as parents and adults, need to take the time to listen and explain to them *why* we've said no. Just think back to how you felt when you would ask "Why?" and you were told "Because I said so." Raising your children will be — and should be — different than how you were raised!

Please understand that this is not something that is going to happen overnight. It is not something that just switches over and suddenly you stop listening to others and just start listening to your inner voice. It is something that needs to be worked on every day. Our mindset is like a muscle; you need to work on it every day to make it stronger. We need to tell ourselves and each other *EVERY DAY* that our children are breathing — and take that as a win. All the other moments, food, gifts, etc., are just icing or the cherry on top. If we all did this, being a mom would be a lot simpler, and would make us much happier moms!

Being a mom isn't about being perfect. It's not about cooking that right food, being the best at the DIYs, having the best and most creative birthday parties, or even about being the parent that's at the school all the time. Being a mom is all about listening to yourself and really listening to your children, because only you can be the best mom for your children — because *they are yours!* No one else will ever fully understand what being the mom to your kids means. So when *YOUR* kid comes to you, hugs you, and says "I love you!" — that's the only validation or "pat on the back" that you need!

Over the years, women have asked me for advice for new moms. Here's the only piece of advice that I will give: I look these women right in the face and say, "Don't forget who you are right now, before you're 'Mom.' You will need this woman as the years go on, so take time with her and make HER the priority, because without this woman — here and now — there would be no 'Mom.'"

CHAPTER 24

Jennifer Weare

FIND JENNIFER: **@HOL_LIFEHUB**

I t's pretty funny how fast I jumped at the opportunity to write about how hard being a mom is, until it came down to writing the damn thing. And then, all of the sudden, I couldn't figure out what to write. I thought I had all the ideas and experiences that would make for a great story, but as soon as I tried to get them out, it didn't feel right. It felt forced, disingenuous, and all around crappy.

So I sat on it. I stepped away from my computer and really reflected on my time as a mom — and what was truly hard. I mean, so many other people have things way harder than me. They deal with things that are really fucking hard, like loss, illness, disasters…and all of the things that are infinitely worse than my motherhood story.

But that's kind of the whole point of this book, isn't it? To show all the various shades of motherhood. The good, the bad, the ugly, and the hard. Maybe my "hard" is totally different from yours, but that's what makes us so special, right? Our own unique motherhood experience can't be packaged up and mass produced. It can't be whittled down into one standard operating guide for all of us to refer to. It's crazy and messy, incredible and wondrous — and an epic adventure of laughter and bullshit. And somehow, through it all, we persevere...because, as moms, we're all connected through our stories of joy and disaster.

I'm not sure why I was drawn to this project, especially since for as long as I can remember, I never thought I would have kids. Not for any particular reason, except for the fact that I never really wanted them. And I'm not even really sure where that came from, but that was me; the girl who didn't want kids.

And then I got married. Fast forward a few years, and here I am. I'm Jen: a married mother of two girls ages eight and eleven, a vegan nutritionist and coach, writing about being a mom. Isn't it funny that I help others shine a light on their own limiting beliefs and BS so they can release them to reclaim their health and happiness, and here I am standing over my own giant pile of crap. What the hell?

Here's the thing...I love my kids more than I ever thought possible, but I haven't always loved being a mom. That's pretty terrifying to say out loud, but it's the truth.

It was only after weeks of contemplation, reflection, and really looking at my entire experience as a mom so far that I realized what made momming so hard for me. It wasn't any particular event or experience; it was something bigger than that. It wasn't something tangible that you could grab or hold onto. It was really just a feeling, that ever-present feeling lingering in the shadows, that somehow puts a toxic spin on just about every moment that I have had as a mother. It was guilt, and man, did my little guilt friend show up right from the start!

My first daughter was born in the hospital on a gorgeous Fall day. I laboured through the night and headed to the hospital around 7:00 a.m. to meet our midwives. Just a couple hours later, she arrived and made me a mother! I was beyond relieved by how straightforward and smooth my first birth experience had been.

I had heard so many tales of horror and epic stories of days in labour, medical interventions, wounds, and scars that I was hesitant to share my own short, uncomplicated, natural birth story. It was like a badge of honour in some of the mom groups that I was a part of. You know, like how guys would stand around and show their scars and tell the tall tales about how they happened. It felt like that. But I didn't survive some horrendous ordeal. It wasn't even really an ordeal. It was one of the most amazing experiences of my life. But then, hearing all of the stories from friends and other moms, I began to feel this weird guilt. Guilt because I hadn't endured days of labour. Guilt because I didn't have to suffer through procedures, and guilt that my baby was happy and healthy. How could I possibly share my experience when everyone else has gone through hell and high water to have a baby? It was like all of the moms were wearing this pin that read "I gave birth and survived" — but I didn't get one.

So naturally, having my second daughter as a planned home birth only seemed to add to the guilt. For the most part, I kept my entire home birth experience on the down low. Somehow, I had developed this belief that sharing my own story would somehow invalidate theirs, and that my very vanilla, g-rated births were not the kind of thing people wanted to hear about. I'm still not entirely sure where this idea came from. Maybe it's that every portrayal of a birth on TV or in movies shows women fighting to survive the birth of their child. Or maybe it was all I heard from women before me; their valiant tales of pregnancy and childbirth. I guess it doesn't really matter where this idea came from, but I've come to realize that it was total bullshit. Keeping my story to myself was a huge disservice to others who might have really needed to hear it — especially to those women who were terrified or overwhelmed and just really needed to hear something good. I've also discovered that sharing our own experiences — good or bad — doesn't take away from someone else's. All of our stories have value, and we need to share them — all of them.

So, now...here I am with a couple of kids, two dogs, a cat, and a house...that stereotypical, middle class family. And with that, I imagined that my husband and I would have date nights and getaways, and our parents would be there to help us navigate raising our kids. It would all be wonderful. Again, my expectations were way off!

Instead, I felt like a walking udder for the first four-ish years of motherhood. I was so lucky to have been able to breastfeed both of my girls for the first couple years of their lives, but there were definitely times where I absolutely hated it. I was the on-call, 24/7 milk machine, which was a blessing and a curse. I loved being able to feed my kids anytime, anywhere, but I also despised it. I hated having to whip out a boob at any moment. I hated feeling like a giant milk bag. I hated feeling invisible but all-important at the same time. And then of course came the guilt. I felt guilty that I didn't love every second of being an udder-on-demand. I felt guilty that I could breastfeed and thought that I should cherish every single second because so many others struggle with it. I felt guilty because sometimes all I wanted to do was go out and have fun without having a baby hanging off of my boob.

Now, don't get me wrong, I am super grateful that I was able to breastfeed, but I'm not ashamed to admit that for me, it didn't always feel like this super amazing, glowy-stardust, motherly experience. I think we need to remind ourselves that being a mom isn't going to feel like sunshine and rainbows 100% of the time...and that's okay!

Sometimes it does, but most times it's gritty and dirty and just plain hard — and we're allowed to feel all of those things, without the guilt.

And then there's the "I'm fine" badge that I wore for a very long time (just my own bullshit, really). I was desperate to have help with cleaning or cooking or just someone to hold a baby, but I was also too damn stubborn to ask for it. And don't forget the guilt!

I felt guilty for wanting to ask for help. I should be able to do it all on my own because that's what "good moms" do. I felt guilty for imposing on the grandparents so I didn't ask for help at a time when I probably could have used it the most. I guess I assumed that people should just show up and offer to help me with anything I needed. Then I wouldn't feel bad for putting them out or not being able to handle everything as a new mom. So of course that ended up morphing into some weird resentment shit based off of completely ridiculous expectations.

It turns out that reflecting on those early days is really uncomfortable. Here I was feeling bitter that my family wasn't there to help as much as I wanted, but all I kept telling everyone was that I was fine. It's fine. Everything is fine. Every moment I was pushing them away, but longing for them at the same time. And, of course, by the time I was willing to admit to myself that it (I) wasn't fine, it was too late.

It seemed like my parents turned into seniors overnight. I don't mean just a number, but I mean they aged really quickly and could no longer handle watching my kids. My dad has a chronic lung disease and gets out of breath just by climbing a couple of stairs. My mom, well, she had her own health scares and I spent nearly two years shuttling her to the emergency department and doctors appointments on a weekly basis. So needless to say, having them watch the kids was out of the question.

I always knew at some point that I would need to help out my parents as they aged. I just hadn't expected that to be while my kids were still small. I didn't think I would be parenting my own parents while still having young kids.

I still feel a lot of guilt and shame around this time and the feelings that I had. I felt guilt that I was not there mentally or emotionally as a wife and a mom during that time. I was so stressed and bitchy and would snap at the drop of a sippy cup. My tank was empty and I dreaded every time the phone would ring, as I knew I would have to rush out to help. I was so bitter and resentful during that period. Why did I have to carry the brunt of helping my parents? Why did I feel like I spent more time at Emerge than with my kids? Why did I have to sit by and watch them suffer? I just remember thinking: *This isn't fair. I have my own stuff. I have kids — and I have needs, too.*

And then, of course, my old friend Guilt shows up and makes me feel like a sack of shit for even thinking those thoughts. How dare I think of my own needs at a time like this? How dare I feel drained and bitter when they ask for help?

I had expectations about how I thought things would go, how I expected others would behave, what I believed about motherhood, and the guilt that I wasn't living up to those super-mom standards. I had subconsciously built up this picture on how I thought things would be, and when real life didn't match up with that weird, unrealistic picture, I felt even more lost, angry, and bitter.

Here I am, sharing some of my darkest thoughts that I've had from motherhood: guilt, shame, resentment, and even anger. I'm pretty sure we all feel this way at one time or another. We all wish we could do those things we used to do pre-kids. We all wish that we were like some TV family with extended family helping out on the daily. We all wish for something. But when all we do is wish, we end up missing what's right in front of us.

I'm so grateful to have my parents and in-laws. I'm grateful to live close enough to help my folks when they need it. I'm grateful that they trust me enough to reach out when they are most vulnerable. I'm grateful for two wonderful children and a supportive husband, and I'm grateful to now realize that sometimes the hardest thing about momming is managing those expectations. Don't get me wrong, being a mom isn't exactly easy, but when we pile on all those bullshit expectations and beliefs on top of it, it makes it even harder.

One of the hardest things I have had to do as a mom is watching my youngest go through an epic emergency surgery ordeal last year. That was not something I was prepared for at all. Watching my child suffer was possibly the worst thing I have ever done in my life.

It's like every parent's worst nightmare; what started off as a stomach ache quickly escalated to a trip to the hospital and emergency surgery. Kids get tummy aches all the time, and my youngest would have one from time to time. They wouldn't last long, until that one… that one that didn't go away.

After waiting forever in the Emergency room with a kid in agony, we were sent back to one of those little rooms and patiently waited for the doctor. After a couple of quick questions and a brief exam, the doctor sent us home, dismissing my concerns and saying it's just a cramp.

But I knew, as a mom, that something wasn't right. She had been moaning and writhing in pain like she was in active labour. I even asked if it might be appendicitis or something more serious, and I was completely brushed off.

So we went home. My poor girl was exhausted and I put her in a nice warm bath to help her feel better. The stomach pains had subsided for a bit, but when dinner came she sat for a few minutes and then just got up and left. I went to go see her and found her curled up in the fetal position on her bed…moaning.

This time, we decided that my husband would take her to the Children's Emergency department at a different hospital. I would stay home with my other daughter until we knew what was going on. It wasn't long before my husband called asking us to come as soon as possible. I could hear her screaming in the background. Trying to drive safely and quickly to reach your hurting child is definitely one of the hardest things to do. When we got there, she was screaming at the top of her lungs in pain. We were that family in Emerge that everyone was trying not to stare at, but was silently thinking, *glad that's not us.*

Once we were seen, they wanted to run a bunch of tests, get her pain meds, and start an IV. They were giving her what they could, but it didn't really help. She was sent for an ultrasound to see if they could find out what was going on inside her little body. The nurse and I had to forcibly pin her down so that they could get clear ultrasound images. All I wanted to do was hold her and comfort her, but instead my heart was breaking as I had to help restrain her and inflict more pain on her aching body.

While we waited for the results, she passed out on the gurney. I thought the pain meds had finally kicked in, but the nurse said "they should have worked ages ago…she's just passed out from the pain." I was crushed, yet somehow I managed not to break down in front of her big sister. We were trying to reassure her that her little sister was going to be okay. Deep down, I wasn't even certain that she would be.

We finally received the results — she had an intussusception. Essentially, she had a blockage in her intestine that needed to be fixed ASAP. They immediately called in the surgical team and got an OR suite ready. We went from a stomach cramp to emergency surgery in just a few hours, but I couldn't think about that. I was laser focused on my daughters and making sure both of them would be okay. She came out of surgery with flying colours, minus a chunk of her intestines and her appendix for good measure.

It took about a month for me to process what had really happened. We all trust our doctors and we believe that they know best, but this wasn't the case this time. I spent a lot of time being angry that we had been brushed off during that first trip to Emerge. I was angry that they didn't believe me when I told them that something was wrong, and that this wasn't normal for my child. I was angry that she could have died if she didn't have surgery. And of course there was the guilt. Why didn't I see this coming? Why didn't I press harder when the first doctor dismissed us? Why hadn't I taken her past tummy aches seriously? Why couldn't I protect her?

It's that Mama Bear stereotype, right? We all have it. We all instinctively protect our young from danger, and we know when something isn't right. Watching your child in pain might be the worst part of motherhood, but then having someone brush off your concerns is just like a kick in the teeth.

After I had cooled off and had a chance to figure out what had happened, I wrote a letter. I wanted to calmly and professionally explain what had happened, and that moms/parents need to have a voice — and be heard — when it comes to the care of their kids.

Even if that first doctor had taken my concerns seriously, it wouldn't have changed the outcome. She still would have needed surgery; however, it could have saved her 12+ hours of pain and suffering. Thankfully, the head of the Emergency department acknowledged that. He also acknowledged that parents are an important key to knowing when something is wrong, and that the doctors need to remember that. I still have the letter and will keep it for my daughter to read one day. Maybe if she becomes a mom it will remind her that she will always know what's best for her kids.

That experience — as shitty as it was — ended up being a wonderful reminder of the power of motherhood. We need to advocate for ourselves and our children, and sometimes, others in a position of authority aren't always right. It's okay to question that. I'm not a doctor, but I'm a mom, and I know when something isn't right with my kids. I'm sure we all have stories of a time when we weren't believed or heard, but we ended up being right. As much as it sucks, it just goes to show that we've all got some magical mom shit going on.

I think that's what makes momming hard sometimes. Every mom has gone through hard stuff, but the thing is — we don't need to compare who has it harder. We get so wrapped up in expectations and beliefs that we forget our own magic...and that guilt's a real bitch.

Our magic creates beautiful humans. Our magic knows when something is wrong with our babes. Our magic gives us the strength to do all that heavy shit. Our magic lets us do what's best for our family. Our magic makes us special and keeps us connected. Yeah, momming is hard, but it's also pure magic.

EPILOGUE

Courtney St Croix

As evidenced by each and every mother's individual story inside the pages of this book, motherhood *does not* come with a manual complete with an alphabetized index for the answers you need, with the instant gratification we're accustomed to. It doesn't come with an off switch, or an easy button, or a cute "what to expect when you're a mother" guide, like we're given when we're expecting. Your personal mothering experience is as unique as each of you are as human beings. It's as distinct as your personal fingerprint; winding and wobbly, intricate and complex, crazy and beautiful...all at the same time.

We often avoid sharing our struggles for fear of appearing ungrateful. We avoid highlighting the difficult pieces of the puzzle, for fear of offending the very people we created or welcomed into our homes with open arms. We wanted this, after all — so we'd better be grateful for every second (You can sense my sarcasm, I hope?).

Yes, we want to be mothers. We dream of it. We desire it. We can't *wait* to become mothers.

Yes, we love our children, to their very core. We love them so much, it hurts.

Yes, we are grateful to have acquired our offspring, no matter what method was employed in order to do so. We are blessed to be able to raise children and help them become beautiful humans.

Yes, motherhood is beautiful. It's fun and life-altering and full of lessons and fabulous.

But it's also…hard AF.

We want you to know: you are not alone.

When you're struggling to be heard among a brood of school-aged children fighting over the remote…we see you.

When you're being constantly interrupted and beckoned to the bathroom to wipe a certain downward-dog-posed toddler's poopy bum… we see you.

When you're spending precious hours in the kitchen making a lovely dinner, only to have your seven-year-old refuse to eat anything other than macaroni and chicken fingers…we see you.

When you're shutting yourself inside your walk-in closet in order to find five minutes to yourself in the vicinity of constant tantrums and bickering…we see you.

When you're feeling guilty and ashamed for *daring* to pour a glass of wine at 1:00 p.m. because you crave something, *anything* that will make you feel a little more numb to the constant demands of the tiny humans in your environment…we see you.

This momming thing, it ain't easy. It's anything *but* easy, and we want you to know that you're not the only one who feels like you're struggling, stressing, losing, or drowning as you attempt to be the best mama you can be for your tiny humans. We want you to know that if you're struggling to find someone to talk to about your challenging experiences, we're here for you.

Momming is hard.

It requires no justification.

It's hard. And that's okay.

It doesn't mean you don't love your children.

It doesn't mean you're a bad mother.

It means…you're human.

If you felt particularly connected to any of the authors inside this project, I urge you to reach out to them and share how you felt reading their chapters. Writing a book is a massive feat — and a huge accomplishment. It takes bravery and strength to share personal details and stories with an international audience. I encourage you to lean into your intuition and reach out to the authors directly if you were moved by — or resonated with — any of the chapters inside this book.

This book is for mothers, by mothers, and we are here to support and connect with you, one reader at a time.

Thank you for picking up this book; for supporting a local author, for listening to our stories, and for seeing yourself inside the pages of this project.

I know it's a cliché , but we are all *truly* in this experience together. It takes a village. We may have completely different experiences, circumstances, and stories, but we can all find a friend in a fellow mother who is just trying her best…and momming *hard*.

Sending you love, light, and appreciation,

CEO, LeadHer Publishing

Other books available from

LEADher.

PUBLISHING

For more information on books, publishing and co-authoring, visit

L E A D - H E R . C O M